BAPTISM, EUCHARIST & MINISTRY 1982-1990

FROM THE LIBRARY OF
THE INSTITUTE FOR
WORSHIP STUDIES
FLORIDA CAMPUS

BAPTISM, EUCHARIST & MINISTRY 1982-1990

Report on the Process and Responses

Faith and Order Paper No. 149
WCC PUBLICATIONS, GENEVA

Second printing September 1992

Cover design: Rob Lucas

ISBN 2-8254-0984-7

© 1990 WCC Publications, World Council of Churches,
150 route de Ferney, 1211 Geneva 2, Switzerland

Printed in Switzerland

Contents

Preface vii

Part One: The Process and the Responses

I. Introduction 3
II. The BEM Process 6
III. The Responses of the Churches 17
    A. General Reactions 17
    B. The Responses to the Baptism Section 39
    C. The Responses to the Eucharist Section 55
    D. The Responses to the Ministry Section 74
    E. The Responses to the Questions in the Preface 89

Part Two: Clarifications and Major Issues for Further Work: Drafts

IV. Draft Clarifications and Comments on Critical Points 107
    A. Clarifications and Comments on the Baptism Text 107
    B. Clarifications and Comments on the Eucharist Text . . . 112
    C. Clarifications and Comments on the Ministry Text 120
V. Major Issues Demanding Further Study: Provisional Considerations 131
    A. Scripture and Tradition 131
    B. Sacrament and Sacramentality 143
    C. Perspectives on Ecclesiology in the Churches' Responses 147

Part Three: Appendices

I: Baptism, Eucharist and Ministry: the Continuing Call to Unity . 155
II: Persons Involved in the Preparation of this Report 159

Preface

> When the Faith and Order Commission of the World Council of Churches completed its work on the *Baptism, Eucharist and Ministry* (BEM) text in January 1982 in Lima, Peru, no one foresaw the interest which the BEM statement would evoke in the Christian community. No one envisaged the impact which it would have within and among churches of such diverse historical origins and such varying traditions. This fruit of many years of ecumenical discussion has become the most widely distributed, translated, and discussed ecumenical text in modern times.
>
> Statement on BEM by the
Faith and Order Commission, Budapest 1989

As a result of this remarkable ecumenical event, many churches requested Faith and Order to prepare a survey of the responses of the churches to BEM, to take up their critical comments, and to give an account of the broad BEM process. The present report (whose preparation is described in chapter I) tries to do this. The report was received by the Faith and Order Commission in August 1989 at Budapest with the understanding that further revision was necessary on the basis of suggestions received before, at or after Budapest, that the last two chapters should be clearly marked as provisional, and that the revised text should be sent to the Faith and Order Standing Commission before publication.

We are happy that we can now offer this report to the churches and all who are interested in learning more about the character and impact of the BEM process and the content and orientation of the responses, and about preliminary clarifications of critical comments and first suggestions for work on some major issues. Faith and Order will take up these issues within the framework of a comprehensive study on ecumenical perspectives of ecclesiology with the aim of achieving a convergence that will be more broadly acceptable than has so far been the case. The report does not mark the end of the BEM process. Rather, we hope that it will serve as a further impetus and encouragement for this theological and spiritual exchange within the Christian oikoumene, so that renewal in the churches and growing communion between them may be granted to us all. The BEM process will also have an impact on the fifth world conference on Faith and Order in 1993 where the churches will have an opportunity for a reappraisal of their ecumenical commitment to unity, mission and service in and for God's world.

Our deep gratitude is due to all who, as a *communio*, have struggled and succeeded with the extremely difficult task of preparing a report of this kind.

John Deschner, Moderator   Günther Gassmann, Director

Commission on Faith and Order
Geneva, Easter 1990

Part One

The Process and the Responses

I. Introduction

1. The *Baptism, Eucharist and Ministry* (BEM) document, adopted by the Faith and Order Commission in Lima, Peru, in 1982, has since then led to a process of discussion, exchange and response which is of major ecumenical significance. The so far 186 official responses of the churches represent an important stage in this process which is still continuing and together they constitute the most representative documentation of the ecumenical thinking of the churches with regard to baptism, eucharist and ministry and wider ecumenical issues connected with them. The present report, after eight years, does not mark the end of this process but seeks to describe some of its major features and results — and the tasks which still lie before us.

2. The multiform and complex diversity of the responses and the wealth of material they contain present a major problem for any summary or evaluation of their content, emphasis and weight. Naturally, the critical comments and suggestions for further clarification occupy more space in the responses than the positive affirmations, which are usually expressed, however, in a clear and encouraging manner. In the preparation of this report Faith and Order has tried to listen to every response, and to respect their particular concerns.

3. A decision was taken to involve a broad range of people in individual research, consultations and group work in the task of reading and evaluating the responses under the leadership of the BEM Steering Group, a sub-committee of the Faith and Order Standing Commission. In order to give a responsible account of what the Commission has perceived by listening to the churches, three larger consultations on the responses to BEM were held: Venice 1986; Annecy 1987; and Turku 1988. A special drafting team met in Paris 1988, Turku 1988, Rome 1988, and together with the Steering Group in Venice 1989. The result of this work was a draft of the present report, which was sent to the members of the Faith and

Order Commission and discussed in groups and plenary sessions at its meeting in August 1989 in Budapest.

4. With the understanding that the structure and content of the draft report would be revised on the basis of written and oral comments made before, at and after the Budapest meeting and that the revised text would be shared with Standing Commission members before publication, it was resolved at Budapest: "The Plenary Commission receives the report on the BEM process and responses. It thanks the churches for their careful, constructive and critical responses, and it encourages them to undertake continued study of BEM with the help of this report. The chapters on 'Elucidations' (IV) [now 'Clarifications'] and 'Major Issues' (V) should be clearly marked in the report as drafts since they will require further work in Faith and Order with the help of reactions." Taking into consideration all the comments received, the BEM Steering Group and drafting team met in Paris from 15 to 21 December 1989 and revised the draft report which was then shared with the Standing Commission before publication.

5. This report is in no way an exhaustive summary and evaluation of the responses of the churches. This would go beyond the possibility and capacity of an ecumenical working group with its limitations in comparison to the kind of research that can be undertaken by scholars and institutes. By documenting the responses of the churches in six volumes, *Churches Respond to BEM*, Faith and Order has also provided the material for more detailed studies on the responses. This material is also a resource for the churches to learn more about the reactions and reflections from other churches. This corresponds to the task of the Commission. The basic conviction that it is not speaking in the name of the churches nor addressing them as a "magisterium" also applies to this report.

6. It is for this reason that this report does not seek to evaluate the responses in a judgmental way but rather intentionally tries to describe as faithfully as possible the churches' convictions and positions. Chapter II looks at the broader BEM process within the ecumenical movement. Central to the whole report is Chapter III which summarizes the main reactions to BEM as a whole, to its three sections and to the questions in the preface to BEM. In chapter IV an attempt is made to take into account the critical remarks in the responses and to clarify and elucidate those statements in the Lima text where it has apparently not been clear enough. Also in this chapter attention has been given to those issues which according to several churches were lacking or not sufficiently dealt with in the text.

7. Finally the report deals with the obvious need to further pursue certain major theological issues which were raised with regard to the Lima document. These issues were taken up during the consultations mentioned above and seen as integral to the follow-up of BEM. On the basis of papers that were given on those occasions the major issues are dealt with in the present report under the heading "Scripture and Tradition", "Sacrament and Sacramentality" and "Perspectives on Ecclesiology" in chapter V. What is said about the three subjects in question should be recognized as a preliminary reflection which requires further theological work in Faith and Order.

8. Taken as a whole, this report on the BEM process and responses should serve as a means of ecumenical "resource-sharing" — a resource-sharing which is facilitated by the Faith and Order Commission as an appropriate instrument for such a theological and spiritual ecumenical exchange among the churches. Rightly understood, the term "ecumenical" always indicates two dimensions — it relates on the one hand to the present churches in their manifold efforts to "grow together in mutual trust" (preface, p.ix) and to be open to each other for their teaching and life, and on the other hand it relates to the teachings and life of the church of all ages from the time of the apostles. The report presented here is intended to point to this double dimension of the churches' ecumenical life and to serve them in their growing communion with one another.

II. The BEM Process

1. The wider context of the BEM document and of the responses

1. The full ecumenical significance of *Baptism, Eucharist and Ministry* can only be grasped if we consider the BEM document and the impressive collection of texts representing the official responses of churches to BEM as results and expressions of broader processes. It is obvious that the achievement in ecumenical convergence which is formulated in the three sections of BEM was only possible within the framework and developments of the ecumenical movement, a new understanding and mutual openness between churches, the theological insights gained in bilateral dialogues and in church union negotiations, the interconfessional exchange in theological work, the experience of common Christian prayer and worship, and joint reflection about common Christian witness and service in response to the problems of humanity in our world. Particularly from the 1961 New Delhi assembly onwards Faith and Order has contributed to the reflection on the nature and goal of the unity of the church (Uppsala assembly 1968, section I, Commission meetings at Louvain 1971, Accra 1974 and Bangalore 1978, consultation at Salamanca 1973 and Nairobi assembly 1975).

2. Likewise the responses of the churches are not to be seen in isolation. They are also, in various degrees, shaped and made possible by this wider context of the ecumenical movement of which the churches are the acting subjects and by which they are, at the same time, deeply influenced in their attitudes and orientations. These responses are also, and again in various degrees, affected by many reflections and discussions on the BEM document within and between churches and in the theological community. The responses asked from the "highest appropriate level of authority" are the official part of this BEM process, but the process itself involves far more than these responses. It is, therefore, appropriate to describe in this chapter this broader BEM process before turning to the official responses themselves.

2. The Lima document: its history and scope

3. The day when the convergence text *Baptism, Eucharist and Ministry* was adopted by the Faith and Order Plenary Commission in Lima, January 1982, will be remembered as an outstanding event. The aim of the text is to be part of a faithful and sufficient reflection of the common Christian tradition on essential elements of Christian communion. It is a first-fruit of the ecumenical pilgrimage towards the goal of lived unity in faith, in sacramental communion, witness and service based on a common understanding of the gospel. As part of a spiritual process of growing together the churches need to further develop the doctrinal convergences registered in the text and to receive and embody them in their lives because they are essential for the unity they seek. This will be an important contribution to enabling them to live in communion with one another in continuity with the apostolic community. The Lima text is thus part of a wider ecumenical process that began many years earlier and is still continuing.

4. It is possible to trace back the roots of this text to the early beginning of the Faith and Order movement itself.[1] The report of the world conference of Faith and Order at Lausanne 1927 already devoted two different sections to the topic of the "ministry of the church" and "the sacraments" — whereas the second world conference at Edinburgh ten years later united them under the general heading "The Church of Christ: Ministry and Sacraments". From a theological and methodological point of view, however, it was not yet possible to overcome the different ways of understanding the sacraments and ministry of the church — these differences were simply listed. The world conference at Lund 1952 considered the themes of the sacraments and the ministry in the context of its sections on "Ways of Worship" and "Intercommunion". Lund signalled the change from a comparative method to a common biblically and Christologically centred reflection and referred to the hermeneutical problem in terms of different "language" and thought-forms concerning the subject under discussion. The report *One Lord, One Baptism*,[2] which was favourably received by the fourth world conference in Montreal in 1963, followed this approach which was further developed by Montreal's clarification of the distinction and relation between Scripture, Tradition and ecclesial traditions.

---

[1] *A Documentary History of the Faith and Order Movement 1927-1963*, ed. Lukas Vischer, St Louis, Bethany, 1963.
[2] London, SCM, 1960.

5. In response to Montreal new studies on baptism, eucharist and ministry were initiated. Their goal was increasingly directed towards "convergence" and "mutual recognition". The full participation of the Roman Catholic Church in the Faith and Order Commission after the Second Vatican Council added further significance to this work. The studies on baptism and on the eucharist were begun at the Commission meeting in Bristol in 1967, while the new study on the ministry started already in 1964. The results of these three studies were presented to the 1971 Commission meeting at Louvain: "Ecumenical Agreement on Baptism", "The Eucharist in Ecumenical Thought" (both were sent to the member churches for study and reaction) and "The Ordained Ministry".[3] Further work on the basis of these reports led to the text on *One Baptism, One Eucharist and a Mutually Recognized Ministry*[4] which was discussed, revised and received at the Commission meeting 1974 in Accra.

6. This text was submitted to the member churches "for consideration and comment" and provoked a process of discussion, evaluation and response. Drawing on these reactions further work led to the convergence document on "Baptism, Eucharist and Ministry" which received its present form at the Commission meeting in January 1982 in Lima. There, the following resolution was passed unanimously: "The Commission considers the revised text on baptism, eucharist and ministry to have been brought to such a stage of maturity that it is now ready for transmission to the churches..."[5] The transmission to the churches was authorized by the WCC Central Committee in 1982. Four questions in the preface to BEM asked the churches to indicate the extent to which they can recognize the "faith of the Church through the ages" in this document, to point out the implications of this text for their ecumenical involvement and for their own life and witness, and to make suggestions for the ongoing work of Faith and Order. The Lima document, together with these four questions has, since 1982, led to reflections and relations whose breadth and intensity is unprecedented in ecumenical history.

7. This short historical review on steps towards convergence up to Lima shows that not only the Lima document but also its forerunners belong to a literary genre of their own which deserves special attention.

---

[3] Cf. *Louvain 1971: Study Reports and Documents*, Geneva, WCC, 1971.
[4] Geneva, WCC, 1975.
[5] *Towards Visible Unity: Commission on Faith and Order, Lima 1982*, Vol. I: *Minutes and Addresses*, Geneva, WCC, 1982, pp.83f.

Obviously a text produced by a single person or a homogeneous group of authors would have had a completely different appearance from that of the BEM document which is the result of many authors coming together from many different churches with their respective confessional traditions. It was rightly called a convergence document because it is the fruit of what all of them, after a long period of dialogue, were now able to affirm together beyond their different theological perceptions. To a certain degree the Lima text was already a text of the churches because they had participated in its formulation through their Faith and Order Commission members and through their detailed comments on preliminary drafts.

3. The published material
8. The final revision and adoption of the BEM text by the Faith and Order Commission in January 1982 was based on the English version of the document. Consequently this version is to be regarded as the standard one. It was first printed by the Publications Office of the World Council of Churches in Geneva and became Faith and Order Paper No. 111. This "Geneva edition" has up to now gone through 24 reprints with a total of 85,000 copies. It is by far the most "successful" publication of the WCC. In addition the English version was reprinted in the United States of America in a large number of copies. In several other countries the English version was reproduced in more limited numbers.
9. In order to enable a wider discussion of BEM, translations into other languages were encouraged and in some cases also supported by Faith and Order. Its secretariat has been informed about 31 translations, some of them only finalized in 1986 and 1987:

Burmese	Hungarian	Polish
Catalan	Icelandic	Portuguese (plus
Chinese	Indonesian	Brazilian edition)
Czechoslovakian	Italian	Romanian
Danish	Japanese	Russian
Dutch	Kiswaïl	Sinhala
Finnish	Korean	Spanish (plus
French	Malagasy	Argentinian edition)
German	Malayalam	Swedish
Greek	Norwegian	Thai
Hindi	Pidgin	Urdu

This is the largest number of translations of any ecumenical document so far. Several of them again received a high circulation which exceeded the usual printing of ecumenical texts. BEM was also reprinted in full or in large sections in several publications and in study material. On the basis of the — incomplete — information available it is assumed that more than 400,000 copies of the full text have been printed and that parts of the text have been printed in more than 150,000 study guides and other material. This makes BEM the most widely distributed text in the history of the ecumenical movement!

10. In order to assist the discussion on BEM, Faith and Order published a volume with theological studies[6] and a study guide.[7] In quite a number of churches and ecumenical bodies study guides were prepared in several languages. They ranged from books to mimeographed material and several of them were produced in large numbers. The — unofficial — Lima liturgy was also printed in several languages and in large numbers. The official responses of the churches and of some ecumenical bodies (through whom groups of churches responded which had not prepared individual responses) were published by Faith and Order in six volumes.[8] A small number of remaining responses will be published in a supplement. Several churches have also published their responses separately.

11. A large number of news items, articles, reports, special editions of periodicals, contributions to collected essays, doctoral dissertations and books have been devoted to the BEM text, the BEM process and the responses to BEM. A preliminary bibliography on BEM prepared by the ecumenical institute of the University of Utrecht lists more than 1,000 items so far.

4. Elements of the BEM process

12. The wide distribution of the BEM text and of study material indicates that the text was not only studied by individuals. Rather, the information available in the form of letters, news items and reports clearly shows that BEM was discussed in thousands of groups on many occasions. These included study groups or seminars in congregations; seminars with special groups like student chaplaincies, women theologians and groups of pastors (both within a particular church or on an ecumenical basis); ecumenical groups or seminars at local or district (province, state)

---

[6] *Ecumenical Perspectives on Baptism, Eucharist and Ministry*, ed. Max Thurian, Faith and Order Paper No. 116, 3rd printing 1985.
[7] William H. Lazareth, *Growing Together in Baptism, Eucharist and Ministry*, Faith and Order Paper No. 114, 7th printing 1985.
[8] *Churches Respond to BEM*, vols I-VI, ed. Max Thurian, Faith and Order Papers 129,132,135,137,143,144, WCC, Geneva 1986-88.

levels; use of BEM in Christian education, adult education and in courses/ seminars in theological faculties and seminaries; discussion on BEM in councils of churches on local, district (province, state), national and regional levels (e.g., Caribbean Conference of Churches, Conference of European Churches, Pacific Conference of Churches); references to BEM in bilateral dialogues and their reports (on national and international levels); consideration of BEM within Christian World Communions; discussion on BEM in theological, liturgical and ecumenical commissions and in bishops' conferences, synodical meetings and other decision-making bodies.

13. Because the controversial issues regarding the understanding and practice of baptism, eucharist and ministry have arisen in European church history, the BEM document found special attention in the churches of Europe, North America and Australasia. However there has also been a remarkable interest in BEM in churches of Africa, Asia, the Caribbean, Latin America, the Middle East and the Pacific, despite the fact that BEM is shaped by a conceptual framework and language that is often strange to them. Furthermore these churches do not have the same technical, financial and administrative possibilities as other churches for facilitating such a broad discussion process. These limitations also explain in part why there have been fewer official responses from these churches in relation to their actual interest in BEM as a means to improve church relations and to clarify the understanding and practice of these basic elements of Christian faith and life.

14. Many of the official responses or the letters accompanying the responses explicitly state that they do not consider the formulation and adoption of a response as the final word in this process. They express the hope that the discussion on BEM will continue and in some cases the response is regarded as a contribution and impetus for such continuation. And indeed, in many situations the discussion on BEM continues in the different forms indicated above — eight years after this document was adopted. It is, therefore, appropriate to speak of a "BEM decade".

5. The impact of the BEM process

15. It is obvious that a broad process of reflection, discussion and reaction like that initiated by and focusing on *Baptism, Eucharist and Ministry* must have had an impact on the churches, their relationships and on the ecumenical movement as a whole. Some of these results of the BEM process can be identified by pointing to "facts". Other implications of the process are less tangible but nevertheless real and confirmed in

letters, reports and personal experiences. Thus, the impact of the BEM process can be summarized under the following aspects:

16. For the first time the ecumenical methodology of communicating to the churches results of theological dialogue in order that they may be discussed, evaluated and responded to has effectively worked on a broad level. This was due to the efforts of churches, ecumenical organizations and the ecumenical commitment of many people. But it was also the result of the recognition that BEM had to be taken seriously as the fruit of a long dialogue between all major Christian traditions, that this text was speaking to essential issues of Christian faith and life and that the aim of BEM was to help remove barriers to full communion between churches.

17. The reality of this broad process is proof that the importance of theological dialogue as one major methodology for the advancement of closer relations between churches has been acknowledged and affirmed by many people in the churches and by the churches themselves. With this renewed confidence in the possibilities of theological dialogue goes the experience that such dialogue and its result will find appropriate attention if it is related to contemporary demands of Christian faith and witness.

18. All this amounts to an ecumenical learning process in which the request to respond to BEM has served as a challenge to clarify one's own position and to open it up to the insights and experiences of others. This has indeed happened and people have been drawn out of narrow or one-sided positions, they have rediscovered forgotten elements of their own tradition and have been changed in their thinking and practice by turning together to "the Tradition of the gospel testified in Scripture, transmitted in and by the church through the power of the Holy Spirit".[9]

19. Being faced for the first time with the request to officially respond to an ecumenical document "at the highest appropriate level of authority" (preface to BEM, p.x) many churches were confronted with questions like the meaning of response and reception, the criteria for responding to an ecumenical text, appropriate structures for elaborating a response, and even, in some cases, who represents their "highest appropriate level of authority". This has led to many clarifications, especially concerning the concept of "reception" where the "classical" concept of receiving dogmatic decisions of a council has been distinguished from a broader concept of a reception process which involves discussion, evaluation and change at all levels of church life leading up to official decisions.

---

[9] Faith and Order World Conference 1963, quoted in the preface to BEM, p.ix.

20. Joint discussions about BEM have initiated many new ecumenical contacts and relationships at local and national levels. It has been taken up and found helpful in church union negotiations. Even in situations with little ecumenical activity so far BEM has served as a first rallying point and has furthered confidence in the seriousness and opportunities of ecumenical dialogue.

21. BEM, and the so-called "Lima liturgy" which has been used in churches and on many ecumenical occasions, have had an impact on liturgical life, studies on worship and official revision of forms of worship in several churches. In addition there have been impulses from the Lima document with regard to spirituality, the social-ethical implications of sacraments and worship, the ecumenical dimension of theological education and, in some cases, the readiness for recognition of sacraments and ministries in other churches.

22. BEM has integrated insights from bilateral dialogues between Christian World Communions. Now, in turn, BEM is used in several of these dialogues as a point of reference and framework for their common orientation. Reports from a number of dialogues refer to BEM when they formulate common affirmations. This is another indication of the complementary relationship between bilateral and multilateral dialogues.

23. In a more general sense BEM has become a point of reference in many ecumenical meetings, statements and addresses of church and ecumenical leaders (e.g., of Pope John Paul II, the archbishop of Canterbury, general secretaries of the WCC and others). These references are used as an indication of the progress of ecumenical dialogue and as an encouragement for further pursuing this process of convergence.

24. The critical comments on BEM and its sections and paragraphs which were made in the process and the official responses are also to be seen as an important result of this ecumenical event. They signal how far the achievements of ecumenical dialogue are acceptable to churches, where the presentation of these achievements requires more clarity and development and which general or specific aspects of baptism, eucharist and ministry require further discussion in the ongoing dialogue.

25. Finally, the official responses themselves, their preparation, quality and number represent a significant result of the BEM process. Never before in history have so many churches reacted at their "highest appropriate level of authority" to an ecumenical document. Their responses provide us with a wealth of material about the ecumenical thinking and expectations of the churches which had not been available before.

6. The official responses of the churches

26. In volumes I-VI of *Churches Respond to BEM* the responses of 179 churches have been published. This number includes (a) churches which have responded together with another church (two Reformed churches in the Netherlands, the Waldensian and Methodist churches in Italy); (b) churches which have responded through their federation (German Democratic Republic); and (c) churches which have not responded individually but through the council of churches to which they belong. Some communions have adopted one common response (Roman Catholic Church, Salvation Army and Seventh Day Adventists) drawing on several reports or responses from their constituency (e.g., a considerable number of reports or responses of Roman Catholic bishops' conferences). Seven responses have not yet been translated into English or have only recently arrived. This brings *the total number of responses to 186*. Of these 55 have come from churches in Africa, Asia, the Caribbean, Latin America and Melanesia. About twenty responses have come from non-member churches of the WCC, including the Roman Catholic Church, whose response was prepared by the Secretariat for Promoting Christian Unity in collaboration with the Congregation for the Doctrine of the Faith. It is the first time that this church has officially responded to an ecumenical document.

27. In addition to the official responses of the churches a considerable number of responses have been received from national and state/provincial councils of churches, confessional and ecumenical organizations, institutes, theological faculties and seminaries, commissions and from many seminars and study groups.

28. The majority of the responses are based on the BEM discussion in the respective churches. Many of them refer to the preceding process of discussion in congregations, theological faculties, commissions, official church bodies, and also in ecumenical meetings. Drafts of the responses have usually been prepared by standing or ad hoc committees of churches or councils of churches. The composition of these groups differed in respect of involvement both of lay and ordained, women and men. In some cases drafts were prepared by some people designated by their church for this purpose. The drafts have been discussed, revised and adopted by the highest decision-making bodies of the churches (holy synod, bishops' conference, assembly, synod, convention, bishop, council, etc.). Some worldwide communions or churches in the same country held consultations before they prepared their responses (cf. e.g., the inter-Orthodox symposium on BEM, Boston, 1985). These different ways in

which the reports were prepared represent important examples for ways of official decision-making and teaching in the churches.

29. With regard to their style, length, methodology and structure, the responses reflect a considerable variety. Some are more general in their comments, others are quite detailed. A number of churches respond to the text as a whole, others deal particularly with those points which are of special relevance for them. Some treat the four questions of the preface separately from the three main sections, others follow the four questions when responding to the sections. Several have developed a particular method for dealing with the contents of the documents, its challenges and its questions. There is a general expression of willingness to be as open as possible towards a better understanding and to mutual agreement. Churches have also frankly stated those points or areas where they still feel particular difficulties for "converging" with other churches. On the basis of their own awareness of the problems they comment and make critical remarks as well as proposals from the perspective of their own tradition, theology and practice.

30. Any evaluation must take into account some factors which have conditioned the production of the responses. Quite a number of churches, for instance, were able to prepare their answers by using the communicating facilities available to them. Others lacked the tools and means of communication to work out a response in order to meet the suggestion for the widest possible involvement of the people of God. Not a few had to struggle in using a foreign language which does not always and easily translate the circumstances, concerns and methods they are familiar with.

31. Another factor relates to responses that come either from one particular church or a worldwide communion. On the one hand, there is a group of churches which belong to the same confessional family existing in different countries and each of which produce their own response — while there is on the other hand just the one response, commonly produced on behalf of all the members of the same worldwide family. For example, compared with the 39 Lutheran responses there is the one common official response from the Roman Catholic Church, and from the Salvation Army and from the Seventh Day Adventists. Of course the numerical strength of the churches also differs considerably. In addition to this there are churches which have been involved in the ecumenical movement for a long time while for others the Lima text was the first opportunity for really entering into the ecumenical dialogue.

32. As the responses are read, it becomes clear that churches have different concerns, interests and priorities. All responses are in different

degrees conditioned by theological and ecclesiological presuppositions relating to their confessional background. Each response is also influenced and shaped by the particular historical and cultural context from which it comes. The churches have tried to give a responsible account of their consideration of the BEM text. However it is not always easy to question one's own tradition on the basis of a text reflecting perspectives other than one's own.

7. Gratitude for a unique process

33. The adoption of the BEM document in Lima by representatives of all Christian traditions after many years of discussion was already a new and major step in the ecumenical pilgrimage of the churches. The dimensions of the exchange and reflection on BEM that followed surprised even those who had hoped that this document might find wide attention. The great number of official responses reflect another unique event in the history of the ecumenical movement. The entire process has brought the churches into a new stage of mutual accountability and is in itself an expression of growth towards visible unity. All this, and especially the general appreciation expressed in the responses, together with the many positive comments on specific points in BEM, and the wider ecumenical impact of the BEM process give us reason for joy and gratitude.

III. The Responses of the Churches

Introduction

The responses of the churches to *Baptism, Eucharist and Ministry* have, in greater or lesser detail, commented on the content of the three sections of the document. Yet nearly all responses have also used this occasion to express the evaluation of the churches in broader perspectives. Thus they comment on the elaboration and adoption of BEM by the Commission on Faith and Order. They refer to the significance of this document for themselves and for the ecumenical movement. They comment on the theological orientation, on the method and the language of BEM. And they often indicate in more general terms their affirmation and criticism of the content of the document as a whole. In connection with these comments, many responses also consider the goal of unity which BEM and the BEM process should serve and on major issues for further work. There are also reflections on the process of reception, and descriptions of this process in the respective churches which led to the formulation of the response. The rich material on these and some other more general issues cannot be adequately summarized in this report. However an attempt is made to present some of the general comments because they provide the framework within which the specific reactions to the three sections of BEM must be seen and understood.

A. GENERAL REACTIONS

1. Appreciation

1. With a few exceptions, all responses applaud the ecumenical achievement represented by *Baptism, Eucharist and Ministry*. Such positive, sometimes enthusiastic, appraisal comes from churches of all

traditions and from all parts of the world. A cross-section of examples suffices to illustrate this. The Roman Catholic response affirms that "BEM is perhaps the most significant result of the (Faith and Order) movement so far" (VI.2). In the response of the Ecumenical Patriarchate of Constantinople the Lima document "is greeted with joy as the fruit of the efforts made during recent decades by the Commission on Faith and Order of the World Council of Churches", and the same response quotes with approval the Inter-Orthodox Preparatory Commission's reference to BEM as "a document which expresses an experience opening up new vistas in the history of the ecumenical movement" (Chambésy, February 1986, para. 7) (IV.l). The Armenian Apostolic Church says: "This initial consensus, which is the gift of the Holy Spirit to the universal church in our time, fills us with hope for solid progress in the coming decades" (II.30). "The synod feels", reports the Malankara Orthodox Syrian Church, "that this is an extremely important milestone in the ecumenical movement" (V.4).

2. The Episcopal Church, USA, states: "We rejoice in the convergence of belief which this document represents and we regard it as a major step which the World Council of Churches has sponsored in the work of healing and reconciliation" (II.58). The Lutheran Church in America "rejoices over the convergence in the text with its promise of the realization of greater visible unity of the church" (I.33). "The Synod of the Reformed Church in Hungary welcomes the Lima document... We are convinced that the Lima document is the best considered and elaborated paper in the whole history of the ecumenical movement in the service of the unity of the church as to these often discussed questions of decisive importance" (V.161). The Church of Jesus Christ of Madagascar affirms: "The BEM document is a work for which we may well praise God. We are very grateful to those who took part in producing it and thank them warmly" (III.186). "The continuing worldwide consultation set in motion by this document is one of the most important ever launched by the WCC," judges the Swiss Protestant Church Federation (VI.75).

3. The United Church of Christ in Japan sees in BEM "a significant contribution, concrete as well as theological, to the unity of the Christian church, calling the various churches into dialogue" (II.287). "Because of the unity already represented in BEM", comments the Christian Church (Disciples of Christ), "and the ways in which differing theological positions are stated, Disciples join other Christians in appreciation for the significance of this document" (I.110). "As United Methodists, we not only rejoice in this unique event in church history, but we praise the

process which has inspired countless Christians — laity, ordained, theological scholars — to study BEM intensely."[1] The Methodist Church of Great Britain testifies: "The Faith and Order Commission has challenged us not to lose heart and shown us a way forward. We respond with gratitude... We are glad that doctrine, so often in the past a cause of dissension, is now proving a means by which we are drawn together" (II.210-211). And the Protestant Methodist Church in the People's Republic of Benin regards BEM as "a text which will always be a milestone in the life of the WCC member churches and the Roman Catholic Church, because blessing it and putting it into practice will be a true sign of the unity we all seek and that the Lord alone can accomplish" (IV.166).

4. The American Baptist Churches in the USA respond: "We give thanks to God for the 'Baptism, Eucharist and Ministry' document — for the co-operation and the dialogue among Christians that made it possible, for the extensive biblical study and the insights which are represented in it, for the way in which many historical confusions and divisions among Christians are addressed in it" (III.258). In the same spirit the Burma Baptist Convention responds with "a spirit of thanksgiving. We are grateful to God for the advent of BEM. Surely it is not by might nor human power that this historic 'ecumenical milestone' has been reached. We express our thanks to all who have committed themselves to this unforgettable ecumenical task and laboured to bring this document into being" (IV.185). "The convergence document is an ecumenical milestone/landmark to churches all over the globe, including our churches here in the Philippines," says the National Council of Churches of that country (V.186). The Moravian Church in America, Southern Province, states: "We welcome and applaud the production of 'Baptism, Eucharist and Ministry' as a most significant ecumenical event... In this process we recognize the work of the Holy Spirit in bringing the church closer together in unity" (II.255). The joint response of Seventh Day Adventists terms BEM as "unquestionably one of the World Council of Churches' most significant publications to date" (II.337). The joint response of the Salvation Army shares "the satisfaction expressed in para. 5 (p. ix) [of the introduction to BEM] regarding 'significant theological convergence' discerned by Faith and Order in the work of the Commission... Our hope would be that this theological convergence will result in renewed and more effective mission and evangelism" (IV.234).

---

[1] United Methodist Church, USA, II.178.

5. In many responses this general appreciation is connected with expressions of thanks and congratulations to the Faith and Order Commission. It is sufficient to quote one voice which is echoed by many others: "We, Christians of the Presbyterian Church in Cameroon, a member of the World Council of Churches since 1961, cannot but praise the efforts of the Faith and Order Commission of the World Council of Churches for this detailed statement on 'Baptism, Eucharist and Ministry'. We praise the persistence with which the Faith and Order Commission has carried on this work since 1927..." (I.81). Together with this goes the commitment to the ongoing work of Faith and Order: "With this response, the Catholic Church wants to encourage Faith and Order to continue its valuable work for seeking unity in faith as the basis for visible unity. We recommit ourselves to this process..."[2]

2. Ecumenical achievement and encouragement of BEM

6. One important element which contributes to the weight of BEM is seen in the fact that it was produced by representatives of all major Christian traditions, and in that sense "the text is already an ecumenical event in itself", as the Evangelical Church of the Lutheran Confession in Brazil observes (II.100). Similarly, the Roman Catholic response remarks: "Theologians coming from groups that were historically often in direct confrontation and disagreement with each other, now together claimed agreement and/or convergence on key issues of faith. This is itself a remarkable achievement" (VI.2). The Greek Orthodox Patriarchate of Alexandria notes: "It is the first time in the history of the WCC that delegates of all the Christian denominations have been able to produce together a joint statement of common doctrine, and this proves the value of dialogue within the WCC" (III.1).

7. Consequently, the fact that BEM represents a convergence of hitherto diverse and even contradictory positions is seen as a major achievement.[3] The Mar Thoma Syrian Church of Malabar affirms: "The ecumenical movement can be proud of the distance travelled towards this agreed statement." But at the same time this response looks to the future: "We hope that the agreement itself will not become an end and that it will help the community of churches to move forward in history in communion with and as guided by the Lord" (IV.13). This historical perspective is

---

[2] Roman Catholic Church, VI.40.
[3] E.g. Lutheran Church of America, I.31; Lutheran Church in Hungary, III.129; Presbyterian Church of Wales, II.166; Evangelical Church of Westphalia, IV.137.

also present in the many responses which regard BEM as an expression of an already achieved closer fellowship and thus as an important step on the way to a fuller manifestation of Christian unity. "The BEM document marks an important stage in church reconciliation dialogue and collaboration," states the Evangelical Church of the Congo (V.168), and the Reformed Church of France follows this up when its National Synod "considers the Faith and Order text to be an important milestone on the ecumenical journey; its production, the thinking it is provoking in the churches, and the conversations arising from it are all part of the process of mutual recognition with a view to the visible unity of the church" (III.163).

8. The interconnection between the BEM text and the reality of the churches on their way towards each other is underlined by the Federation of Evangelical Churches in the German Democratic Republic: "Manifestly these texts are not merely the products of discussions by expert theologians, they are also, and primarily, the expression of the churches' growing together — in their life and in spiritual fellowship — as this has been achieved in the ecumenical movement of the twentieth century" (V.119). And we may end with once again a further quotation which looks to the future. The Baptist Union of Great Britain "welcomes it (i.e. BEM) as a notable milestone in the search for sufficient theological consensus to make possible mutual recognition among separated churches" (I.70).[4]

9. In this future-oriented perspective responses see in BEM a solid basis for ecumenical progress as this is expressed by the Presbyterian Church of Rwanda: "We are extremely appreciative of the ecumenical effort which led to the existence of this document. We are convinced that theological foundations such as this provide a sound approach to the ecumenical future of the churches" (III.185).[5] "It is to be hoped", concludes the response of the Finnish Orthodox Church, "that it will also be a source of inspiration and hope for the new strivings of the ecumenical movement for the unity of the church in the years to come" (II.29). In this

---

[4] Similar statements to those in this paragraph were made by, for example, Evangelical Church of the Augsburg Confession in Alsace and Lorraine, III.145; American Lutheran Church, II.84; Presbyterian Church, USA, III.204; Orthodox Church in America, III.15; Finnish Orthodox Church, II.24; Waldensian Evangelical Church of the River Plate, IV.18-19.

[5] Cf. also e.g. Bulgarian Orthodox Church, II.15; Evangelical Church of Kurhessen-Waldeck V.94; Church of Norway, III.185.

ongoing work BEM has, as the Ecumenical Patriarchate observes, "already become a point of reference in ecumenical gatherings, as well as in the wider sphere of co-operation and mutual acquaintance of Christians belonging to the divided churches"(IV.3).[6]

10. Thus, for the Evangelical Church of the Augsburg Confession in Alsace and Lorraine, "the Lima document is undoubtedly a document of hope" (III.147). This note of hope and encouragement also resounds in other responses. The Romanian Orthodox Church, for example, sees in BEM "a proof of confidence and also hope and a reason for the continuation of the efforts to be made with fraternal love with the view of achieving the unity of the church" (III.14).[7] The process of response to BEM is also experienced as such an encouragement: "We are also appreciative of the objectivity and openness displayed in soliciting responses," observes the Moravian Church in Jamaica (V.169), and the Melanesian Council of Churches takes this one step further: "Our churches in Melanesia feel that they can be part of the movement towards greater unity among Christians by responding to BEM" (V.179).

3. Theological orientation of BEM

11. Another group of comments which undergirds appreciation of the Lima document refers to the role of biblical and historical study and theological and doctrinal reflection as well as to basic theological orientations of the document. Especially Lutheran responses echo the statement of the Evangelical Lutheran Church of Finland: "The document demonstrates convincingly how important questions as to the content of doctrine and faith are, from the point of view of both the unity of the church and also of church life... Also as a guide to the whole ecumenical movement the document is important in this sense. For it demonstrates how making a deep study of faith and doctrine can also make a contribution to the church's diaconal service in the world" (III.126).[8] The Church of Scotland refers to the "disciplined nature of the work that went into it which combined biblical, systematic, theological and liturgical studies" (I.88).

---

[6] Cf. also United Free Church of Scotland, IV.183: "a reference point for future discussion".
[7] Cf. also United Church of Christ, USA, II.328; Uniting Church in Australia, IV.154; Federation of Evangelical Churches in the GDR, V.151.
[8] Cf. e.g. Lutheran Church-Missouri Synod, III.132; American Lutheran Church, II.80; Lutheran Church of Australia, II.87; Evangelical Church of the Augsburg Confession in Austria, IV.17.

This has, according to the Christian Church (Disciples of Christ), "generated a new appreciation and much-needed interest in serious theological reflection among Disciples regarding fundamental aspects of our faith" (I.113).

12. With regard to the theological orientation of BEM, the Orthodox responses recognize in BEM, with the words of the Russian Orthodox Church, "a step towards greater catholicity, i.e., greater proximity to the apostolic tradition, to the faith and practice of the early church" (II.5).[9] Reformation and Free churches point to "the extensive biblical study" underlining the statements in BEM.[10] Concerning basic theological orientations of BEM, the Presbyterian Church of Canada affirms: "The theological emphasis is certainly Trinitarian and there is an authentic Christological focus. We welcome also the significant place given throughout to ethical, eschatological and missionary themes as well as the way in which the power of the Holy Spirit is consistently recognized" (II.152-53).[11]

4. Challenge to renewal

13. The significance of BEM is also — and emphatically — seen in its challenge to the churches to reconsider their own positions of faith and practice and to open them up to the wider horizon and enrichment offered to them by the insights and experiences of other churches. Accordingly, the Uniting Church in Australia sees the churches "challenged to think again about their own views, the reasons for which they are held and their continuing significance, and thus to contribute to an ongoing dialogue that anticipates that all the churches will go beyond otherwise entrenched positions" (IV.154).[12] According to the Presbyterian Church of Korea the "theological document achieved by the Faith and Order Commission is regarded to be of vital importance and significance to the Korean church not only for her ecumenical worship, witness and service, but also for her ecclesiastical identity in the midst of a rapidly changing technological

---

[9] Cf. also Ecumenical Patriarchate of Constantinople, IV.3; Bulgarian Orthodox Church II.15; Finnish Orthodox Church, II.25.
[10] American Baptist Churches in the USA, III.258; cf. also Evangelical Lutheran Church in Canada, II.102; Reformed Church of America, II.141; Reformed Church in Hungary, V.161.
[11] For similar references to the Trinitarian and Christological emphasis see e.g. Roman Catholic Church, IV.4; Evangelical Lutheran Church in Canada, II.102.
[12] Cf. e.g., United Methodist Church, USA, II.178; Union of Welsh Independents, III.283; Moravian Church in Great Britain, III.284; Church of Sweden, II.125.

society" (II.160). Non-sacramental communities,[13] too, have accepted the challenge to reflect upon baptism, eucharist and ministry, and even though they have reaffirmed their own position they have expressed their willingness to continue to participate in the common ecumenical endeavour.

14. Integral to this challenge is the recognition that the Lima document, according to the Protestant Church in Sabah, "helps us to see our neighbouring churches in a new light and indicates that... there is nothing theologically relevant which should keep us from working towards unity and united witness" (VI.132). In this way BEM "broadens our horizon; we learn from the conceptions of other churches".[14] This is spelled out by the Evangelical Lutheran Church in Bavaria when it affirms that "the convergence texts can help us to rediscover theological insights and forms of ecclesial practice which have retreated into the background or which have been forgotten and to make them fruitful for the present... The convergence texts open up for us the wealth of theological knowledge and the variety of worship of other churches. They inspire us to accept new and unaccustomed elements and to give a more lively shape to our church life and for this we are grateful" (IV.24-25). In the same vein a united church appreciates "the wealth of thought-provoking ideas from other churches which can help enliven our worship services and liturgy. We see in this text an impressive description of the dynamic way in which the churches are drawing closer together."[15] And this is a reminder for the United Church of Canada, "that we are not alone, but part of a world fellowship of believers in Christ's name" (II.286).[16] "However", says the Old Catholic Church of the Netherlands (mimeographed paper), "this enrichment is a painful process, for every partner may have to sacrifice or at least to relativize something of his own at the same time, in order that a new general Christian identity can come into being, not in a super-church, but within a lasting diversity of confessions which know that they are no longer separate."

15. That this "learning process" through consideration of BEM should have concrete consequences for the renewal of theology and practice in

---

[13] The Salvation Army, IV.235; Society of Friends, Canada, III.301.
[14] United German Mennonite Congregations, VI.123.
[15] Evangelical Church of Westphalia, IV.137.
[16] This enrichment is also mentioned by, e.g., United Methodist Church, Central/Southern Europe, II.200; Evangelical Lutheran Church of Denmark, III.107; Evangelical Lutheran Church of Iceland, IV.57; American Baptist Churches in the USA, III.258.

the churches is affirmed in many responses. The Holy Catholic Church in Japan (Anglican) states: "We can find in this text a pertinent guideline for a revitalization of worship, Christian education, moral and spiritual life in each church" (III.99). The Evangelical Lutheran Church of Denmark says that "we are willing to be inspired by the declaration in the teaching and theological training of our own church and in endeavours towards church and liturgical renewal, and to allow the declaration to correct our view of baptism, eucharist and ministry of the other churches" (III.107).[17] Several churches refer in this context also to positive experiences with the so-called "Lima liturgy"[18] while the whole Lima process has been for the Church of the Brethren in the USA "an experience of renewal as Brethren have asked how diverse understandings and expressions of baptism, eucharist and ministry may be life-giving for all members of Christ's body" (VI.112).

5. BEM as basis for ecumenical relations and dialogue

16. The Lima document and the process of learning and renewal it can initiate leads churches closer to each other. Thus BEM, according to the Armenian Apostolic Church, "makes us feel closer to traditions and confessions other than ours in the apostolic faith and makes us realize more vividly our fundamental unity with them in orthodoxy and orthopraxis" (II.30). The Roman Catholic Church states that "despite our continuing divisions, a real, though imperfect communion already exists between divided Christians. The BEM text explains the baptismal basis of this communion that already exists" (VI.38). In a similar way the Evangelical Lutheran Church of France says that BEM "offers real convergence which can create and strengthen a deep ecclesial fellowship between different confessions" (III.158). In order to be able to move forward to full communion or visible unity, BEM is regarded not only as an impulse for new encounters and relations but also as a helpful instrument for strengthening church relationships and for further ecumenical conversations on different levels: "The Lima document may serve as a good basis of ecumenical dialogue on the international as well as on the national and local level," affirms the general synod of the

---

[17] Similar views are expressed by, e.g., Anglican Church of Canada, II.47; Church of Jesus Christ of Madagascar, III.186; Church of North India, II.69-70; United Church of Christ, USA, II.325; United Church of Christ in Japan, II.290-291.
[18] E.g. Remonstrant Brotherhood, II.304; Evangelical Church in Berlin-Brandenburg (West Berlin), VI.58; Church of North India, II.69; Church of Norway, II.122.

Church of Norway (II.105).[19] "We accept the value of the paper as a resource document for use in our own bilateral conversations," states the Anglican Church in Australia (II.35).[20]

17. In this connection the complementarity between bilateral and multilateral dialogues is affirmed. The (Anglican) Church in Wales expresses this in the following way: "This remarkable multilateral text is a reminder of the oneness of the ecumenical movement and provides a context in which to view the convergences in any of the bilateral dialogues" (III.80).[21] The Evangelical Church of Lutheran Confession in Brazil views BEM "as a useful study document for studies not only at the level of international commissions but much more at the level of concrete relations between the churches locally... The text will, moreover, help to strengthen relationships and dialogue with other churches to the extent that... attempts are made to reach official agreements, even partial agreements, between the churches concerning the implications of the text, such as, for example, mutual recognition of baptism, etc." (II.101). The testimony of the United Church of Christ in the USA is confirmed by other churches in similar unity endeavours: "We find our experience as a 'united and uniting church' affirmed by the kindred struggle for wholeness and inclusiveness that we recognize in the document" (II.326).[22] And the Evangelical Lutheran Church of Württemberg clearly indicates a consequence which is, finally, intended by BEM: they are ready to accept "the baptism, eucharist and the ordination of those churches which can agree with us on the fundamental issues of these convergence statements" (V.31). Cf. also part E of this chapter: "2. Responses to the Second Question".

18. "The Church of North India sees this text as more than a theological document in an academic sense. It is a text which has to be received with thanksgiving, and used prayerfully. Not as a final and perfect statement of the truth, but as a door that invites us to pilgrimage into unity in Christ" (II.70).

---

[19] The Evangelical Church of the Augsburg Confession of Alsace and Lorraine sees BEM as "an invitation to dialogue with other churches" and as "a fruitful instrument for the ecumenical dialogue", III.146.

[20] A few other examples of the same position: Anglican Church of Canada, II.47; Evangelical Lutheran Church in Brunswick, VI.44; Evangelical Church of the Czech Brethren, IV.110; Churches of Christ in Australia, II.274.

[21] Cf. also Anglican Church of Canada, II.37; Roman Catholic Church, VI.37.

[22] Cf. also Church of the Province of New Zealand (union negotiations), II.68; Presbyterian Church of Wales (covenant negotiations), II.166.

6. Method, terminology and language of BEM

19. Many responses comment on formal aspects of BEM like methodology, approach, terminology and language — aspects which also have implications for content and thus for the acceptability of certain statements. These comments are summarized under two main categories which pertain (a) to approach, methodology and style, and (b) to terminology and language.

20. With regard to (a) *methodology*, affirmative comments clearly prevail. Thus, the Russian Orthodox Church says: "The Lima document is well-structured methodically. There is a good balance between the agreed and the disputed material, subject to further clarification. The tone of both the paragraphs and commentaries is both descriptive and positive. The statement does not appear to be designed to exhort or edify the churches concerning this or that tradition or practice" (II.6). The (Anglican) Church of Ireland finds "Lima a very positive document, admirable in its comprehensiveness, its honesty of approach, and its economy of style... It does not attempt to cover over differences, nor is it superficial in searching for areas of agreement" (I.63). The Methodist Church of Great Britain judges that "the approach adopted by the Faith and Order Commission is judicious and encouraging... the strength of the text lies in the fact that it recognizes diversity while at the same time looking for and revealing convergence" (II.211). "We welcome the approach the document takes," responds the Baptist Union of Scotland, "inasmuch as it is not a belligerent exchange of ideas from fixed positions but more a common search for 'the Tradition of the Gospel testified in Scripture, transmitted in and by the Church through the power of the Holy Spirit' (p.ix)" (III.232).[23]

21. Not all responses concur, however, with these positive evaluations. Thus, the Evangelical-Methodist Church in the Federal Republic of Germany and West Berlin notes that "diverging positions were simply placed side by side. Controversial points were neutralized, concealed or completely silenced through variously explicit formulations... Thus the danger arises that statements feign more unity than actually exists. On the other hand, through ecumenical conversations seeking understanding of such statements, the possiblity of reaching more agreement can also arise" (IV.173). The Evangelical Church of the Augsburg Confession of Alsace and Lorraine sees in BEM an attempt "to press forward beyond the

---

[23] For similar positive reactions, cf. e.g. Anglican Church of Canada, II.38; Lutheran Church-Missouri Synod, III.132; Lutheran Church of Australia, II.87.

different ecclesial traditions. It is therefore a compromise statement which is not without its ambiguities and consequently requires a certain number of clarifications" (III.145).

22. The word "ambiguity" in this last quotation is frequently mentioned with regard to (b) *terminology/language* of BEM. The American Lutheran Church judges that "the language of the text is frequently ambiguous, open to a number of possible interpretations... It is not clear where the document seeks to be descriptive and where it seeks to be prescriptive. This in turn fosters confusion about the intended purpose of the text, and concern about 'papering over' significant differences" (II.80). "The language is in places obscure and unfamiliar," summarizes the Presbyterian Church of Ireland (III.221). Such critical comments, which are shared by other responses,[24] refer also to the need for more clarification with regard to certain terms like "eucharist" or "sign". The United Church of Christ, USA (II.327), the United Methodist Church in the USA (II.197-198), and the United Church of Canada (II.285) refer to insufficiently employed "inclusive language" in the text while, on the contrary, the Church of England notes "that the language of the Lima text is inclusive" (III.78). Other responses speak of a "new theological vocabulary"[25] or "welcome the approach and language of the Faith and Order Commission"[26] or find that "the statements in the text... express the meaning in new and acceptable terminology helping the CNI and other churches to think afresh, to think and to grow together".[27] These different evaluations point both to the difficulties inherent in the formulation of ecumenical texts and to the different ways in which such texts are perceived according to diverse presuppositions.

7. BEM and contemporary and social-cultural contexts

23. A number of responses comment on the relation of the Lima document to specific contemporary social and cultural contexts. Here, perhaps the strongest critique comes from the United Church of Canada (which has, of course, also many positive things to say about BEM). This church finds that BEM "suffers as a contemporary affirmation of the ecumenical church precisely because of its lack of sensitivity to context".

---

[24] C.f. e.g. Church of Norway, II.122; Presbyterian Church in Canada, II.153; Union of Evangelical Free Churches (Baptists) in the German Democratic Republic, IV.191.
[25] Roman Catholic Church, VI.4.
[26] Anglican Church of Canada, II.38.
[27] Church of North India, II.69.

Such "lack of contemporaneity in the text" is seen in the fact that "the text is decidedly patriarchal in tone", that BEM does not recognize "that our affirmations of faith are intrinsically social statements, and not simply a prolegomenon to social ethics", and that in a world of many religions and ideologies BEM fails to acknowledge "that the water is poured, the bread is broken, the cup shared, the ministry called forth in a world of many sacraments and many ministries, not all of which are ours" (II.285-286). Also three responses from churches in Latin America and Asia include critical comments along the lines of the findings of the United Church of Christ in Japan that BEM "cannot be said to be completely relevant to our situation. In general it comes across to us as strongly influenced by the values of the so-called 'Christian world' of Europe and North America. We realize that an effort was made to give consideration to so-called 'younger churches' but it is highly dubious that BEM reflects the issues and tasks of churches in the third world as symbolized by such meeting places as Accra, Bangalore, and Lima" (II.288).[28]

24. The Melanesian Council of Churches states "that many of the theological problems addressed in BEM seem foreign to us, since they arise out of the history of Christianity in Europe... However, we realize that missionaries, in bringing us the Christian faith, also brought divisions which separate Christians throughout the world. In doing our part to help heal these divisions, we hope to grow in communion with our partner churches overseas and with Christians in other developing countries whose problems are similar to ours" (V.180). Such a "mediating position" is even more strongly expressed by the affirmation of the Burmese Baptist Convention: "We do not feel that we are responding to a 'foreign' document... even though we are Burmese, we are at the same time members together in the one family of God on earth" (IV.185). And most will agree with the request of the Presbyterian Church in Cameroon that in view of the different cultural contexts in which the church lives "variety and diversity will be tolerated, and this too will become an expression of the richness of the church's way of living out its belief" (I.83).[29]

8. Content of BEM: major points of criticism

25. Within the framework of their general assessment of *Baptism, Eucharist and Ministry* many responses contain critical comments on

---

[28] Cf. also Waldensian Evangelical Church of the River Plate, IV.118; Theological Committee of the National Council of Churches in Korea, VI.134.
[29] Cf. Evangelical Church of the Congo, V.168.

major emphases or insufficient emphases of the content of BEM and its theological orientations. These critical observations are taken up in chapters IV ("Clarifications") and V ("Major Issues") of this report, but it may be helpful to summarize them here as well.

26. In a more general sense Orthodox responses contain critical comments which can be summarized by the finding of the Finnish Orthodox Church that "some parts of the document include theological terminology, categories and problematics of the Roman Catholic and Protestant churches of the West. In most cases the way the common faith of the undivided church is expressed is strange for us" (II.25). On the other hand, a number of Reformation and Free churches observe "that the general direction of this report has been greatly determined by churches with a strong liturgical tradition emphasizing the sacraments and the ministry". This finding of the Mission Covenant Church of Sweden (II.316) is echoed by other responses which speak of a too "catholic" or "high church" orientation of BEM[30] or find that "one cannot overlook the insufficient appraisal of the discoveries of the Reformation" (Evangelical Church of the Augsburg Confession in Austria, IV.20). Among this group of critical comments the strongest ones come from the Waldensian and Methodist Churches in Italy. Their synod points out, together with differentiations and affirmative remarks, that BEM "indicates a convergence in a sacramental and clerical direction which is opposite to the direction in which the gospel calls the church in its witness in the world" and that "this ecumenical document centres the faith, communion and Christian witness not on God and the gospel, but rather on the church as a sacred structure that has and gives guarantees of the Spirit's activities through a caste endowed with priestly powers, mediatorial, and representing the divine" (Ministry, paras 11,14,17) (II.245-246).

27. Specific critical issues mentioned by Reformation and Free churches are enumerated in the response of the American Lutheran Church which misses an emphasis on the "centrality of justification by grace through faith", on the "centrality of the word and proclamation", and on the "dynamic of sin and grace". In addition, "the text appears to regard certain periods of history as normative for the faith... the text is heavily inward-directed rather than mission-oriented" (II.81). These points reappear in other responses, even though the way in which they are formu-

---

[30] C.f., e.g., United Church of Canada, II.284; American Lutheran Church, II.81; United Church of Christ, USA, II.327; Presbyterian Church in Ireland, III.221.

lated differs considerably. Accordingly several responses raise the question of criteria or norms for the faith and find that BEM places too much weight on tradition.[31] Some state that scripture is the only norm,[32] while others request further work on the relation between Scripture and Tradition, word/gospel and Tradition[33] (cf. V. "Major Issues", part A). The Presbyterian Church of Wales, however, states: "The understanding of tradition as referring back to canonical scripture itself for sanction, while recognizing that scripture itself is both the product and authority of tradition, is a position we find both helpful and challenging" (II.166). Some responses find a too heavy accent on ecclesiology (including a certain sacramentalism and clericalism) or on the role of the church in the sacraments and thus in God's saving action in Jesus Christ.[34] There is not sufficient attention given to the gospel, the relation between word of God and sacrament, to soteriology and to mission.[35] BEM is also regarded by two responses as rather protective, conservative, ahistorical and thus not sufficiently related to the concern for the unity and renewal of humankind,[36] while another response clearly sees such a relation in BEM.[37]

9. Content of BEM: recognition and acceptance

28. All the responses welcome the fact that BEM has been presented as a "convergence document". As noted earlier, this convergence on the understanding of baptism, eucharist and ministry, which also includes agreements, is usually considered as an important achievement for the ecumenical movement, for the self-understanding and renewal of the churches, and for further steps towards visible unity. At the same time and frequently by the same responses the term "convergence" is welcomed because it does not claim too much. The term "convergence" clearly signifies for them that a full consensus has not yet been reached on

---

[31] E.g. Lutheran Church-Missouri Synod, III.141; Evangelical-Methodist Church in the Federal Republic of Germany and West Berlin, IV.174.
[32] E.g. Evangelical Methodist Church in the German Democratic Republic, IV.167.
[33] Reformed Church of France, III.163-164; Evangelical Church in Hessen and Nassau, IV.128.
[34] Evangelical Church of the Lutheran Confession in Brazil, II.100; United Church of Canada, II.284.
[35] Evangelical-Lutheran Church in Canada, II.102; Swiss Protestant Church Federation, VI.79.
[36] United Church of Christ, USA, II.327; United Church of Christ in Japan, II.290.
[37] Reformed Church in Hungary, V.161.

all points they consider important.[38] Moreover, they could not receive all the statements presented in BEM. In this sense, BEM as a convergence document can be seen as a stage or step in a process.

29. Related to this is the fact that for some churches such convergences, if accepted by the churches, are already sufficient for mutual recognition of sacraments and ministries (as some responses affirm) while for other churches these convergences do not yet provide a basis, for example for intercommunion, before a fuller and more comprehensive consensus has been reached.[39] It seems to be necessary to clarify further what kind of agreement would be required and sufficient and what degree of diversity would be acceptable for the unity we seek. The responses reveal open questions or differing positions on these issues.

30. Many responses contain general evaluations of the content of the Lima document. Most of these are formulated as a response to the question in the preface to BEM concerning "the extent to which your church can recognize in this text the faith of the Church through the ages". The formulation of this question has created some difficulties (cf. V. "Major Issues", part E). Some churches have understood it in the sense that the tradition or the church is made the norm of the faith while others have found the formulation not very precise. The Evangelical Baptist Union of Italy (mimeographed document) questions even the presupposition underlying the first question and points to the Reformation which marks a discontinuity in relation to the faith of the church through the ages. On the whole, however, the responses reveal that the intention of this question, which should have been made more explicit, has been appreciated, namely "to challenge the churches to look beyond their own tradition when evaluating and responding to BEM" (Faith and Order consultation on BEM, Venice, 1986). Other responses use other expressions like the "apostolic faith" or "the faith of the church" or state in more general terms their evaluation of the content of BEM. Only a very few arrive at the conclusion that, despite positive elements in BEM, "it is not... a statement which we can unequivocally accept as expressing adequately the basic elements of our faith and understanding".[40]

---

[38] Cf. e.g. Romanian Orthodox Church, III.4; Evangelical Church of the Lutheran Confession in Brazil, II.99; Swiss Protestant Church Federation, VI.75.
[39] Russian Orthodox Church, II.5; Ecumenical Patriarchate of Constantinople, IV.3.
[40] Presbyterian Church of Canada, II.158; similar: Baptist Union of Scotland, III.233; Union of Welsh Independents ("only to a very limited extent does BEM express it"), III.382.

31. Quite a number of responses come, despite their critical questions and concerns, to the general conclusion of the Evangelical Lutheran Church in Canada: "We affirm that we can recognize in this text the faith of the church through the ages" (II.104).[41] Or they formulate it, like the Old Catholic Church in Switzerland, in this way: "We approve those texts as a whole and declare our conviction that they do not contain anything that would contradict the faith of the church through the ages" (V.8; cf. also Old Catholic Church in Germany, mimeographed document). The General Assembly of the Church of Scotland recognizes in BEM "an up-to-date statement of the 'faith of the church through the ages'" (I.86). Most of these responses, however, express this recognition with a certain reserve (because of their critical comments on individual points in the three texts). Thus, the motion carried by the General Synod of the Church of England was: "That this Synod to the extent described in GS.661 recognizes in 'Baptism, Eucharist and Ministry' the faith of the church through the ages" (III.79). Other responses express this reserve by formulating their recognition "subject to the comments made in this response" (Anglican Church of Australia, II.35), by recognizing in BEM "a high degree of convergence in expressing the faith of the church through the ages on these matters" (Anglican Church of Canada, II.47) or "major elements of the faith..." (Episcopal Church, USA, II.62). The Church of Norway recognizes the faith of the church "in a great number of statements" (II.122) and the Methodist Church of New Zealand recognizes "the core of the faith..." (I.79). The Methodist Church of Great Britain says that if the question (of the preface) is interpreted prescriptively "our response to the question is basically positive" (II.213). The Baptist Union of Denmark responds: "We recognize in the document 'the faith of the church throughout the ages' though we find this expression more a description of the creative power of the ecclesiastical

---

[41] Holy Catholic Church in Japan (Anglican): "an appropriate expression of the faith of the church handed down through the ages from the apostles' time", III.99; Church of the Province of Southern Africa: "an expression of the faith..." III.101; Church of the Province of New Zealand, II.64; Evangelical Lutheran Church of Denmark: "an expression of the faith..." III.107; Christian Church (Disciples of Christ): BEM "reflect the faith...", I.113; Christian Church (Disciples) in Canada: "an expression of the faith..." and "fair representation of the faith of the apostolic church", III.264 and 266; United Church of Christ, USA: "an expression of the faith...", II.334; Church of Christ in Thailand: "as expressing the faith...", V.174; Moravian Church in America, Southern Province: "We most emphatically recognize in 'Baptism, Eucharist and Ministry' an expression of the faith...", II.256; Congregational Union of Scotland: "reflect the faith...", II.314.

tradition than the norm of confession which alone can be found in the canonical scriptures" (III.247). The Northern Province of the Moravian Church in America asserts "that the BEM text is an expression of the faith of the church through the ages. However, we see it as an *a priori* insufficient expression of that faith, standing in need of constant testing" (II.262).

32. When the Lutheran Church-Missouri Synod says that "at many points the 'faith of the Church through the ages' is clearly set forth" (III.141), this combination of affirmation and reserve is related by some responses to the three sections of BEM. Thus the Roman Catholic Church finds "the text on baptism to be grounded in the apostolic faith received and professed by the Catholic Church", it "can recognize in the statement on the eucharist much that corresponds to the understanding and practice of the apostolic faith, or, as is said in the document, the faith of the church through the ages", and it appreciates that the presentation of the ministry text "goes in the direction of the major lines of what we recognize 'as the faith of the church through the ages'" (VI.9, 16 and 25). The Reformed Churches in the Netherlands/Netherlands Reformed Church recognize in the sections on baptism and eucharist "fundamental elements of the church's faith through the ages... In the report on ministry we discover less of these fundamental elements" (IV.108-109). The judgment of the Mission Covenant Church of Sweden goes in the same direction: "... our church identifies itself most readily with the texts about the eucharist and baptism, whereas the report on the ministry in many ways seems foreign to us" (II.315). The distinction made in these three responses between the baptism and eucharist section on the one hand and the ministry section on the other hand (although for different, even opposite reasons) is shared probably by the majority of the responses.

33. Quite a number of other responses express their general recognition or agreement, with or without reservations, in terms of "the faith of the church" or "the apostolic faith". Accordingly, the Presbyterian Church in Cameroon recognizes "in the text the expression of the belief of the Christian church concerning the central rites of baptism, eucharist and ministry..." (I.82), while the Finnish Orthodox Church states that "in many parts of the document the faith of the church has been clearly expressed in the language of traditional theology" (II.25). "Lutherans are able to approve the document as a witness to the apostolic faith, while also stating that there is more of the Tradition than is set forth in 'Baptism, Eucharist and Ministry'," affirms the Lutheran Church in America (I.34). The North Elbian Evangelical Lutheran Church approves

"these texts in principle because in their fundamental affirmation we clearly recognize not only the scriptural basis which our Reformation approach to doctrinal statements requires but also the tradition of the apostolic faith through the ages as formulated in the ancient creeds and adhered to in our confessions of faith" (I.40). And the Federation of Evangelical Churches in the German Democratic Republic responds: "We can recognize the present texts on baptism, eucharist and ministry as a testimony to the Christian, apostolic faith, in accordance with holy scripture" (V.147).

34. Other responses use different expressions for their recognition, acceptance, agreement, and reception with regard to BEM. The Church of North India recognizes in BEM "the core of the Christian faith relating to these areas of life" (II.69). The general assembly of the Presbyterian Church of New Zealand "gives general approval of its contents as an adequate statement of the meaning of baptism, eucharist and ministry for the church today" (II.175). "The Protestant Methodist Church in the People's Republic of Benin accepts without reservation the Lima document on 'Baptism, Eucharist and Ministry'" (IV.166). The Czechoslovak Hussite Church finds in BEM "much of what has constituted the life of the Christian church ever since its apostolic beginnings" (II.299). The Mar Thoma Syrian Church of Malabar expresses "general agreement with the statements of the paper" (IV.7), while still other churches use similar formulations as the ones quoted here.[42]

10. BEM and the unity we seek

35. In their general observations and reflections many responses consider the goal of unity to which BEM and the BEM process are directed. They also raise questions of methodology which are implied in the ecumenical task of manifesting the unity of Christ's church. Quite a number of responses refer to the goal in terms of "visible unity" or a "visibly united church" (Church of England, III.33), a unity founded "in the evangelical, catholic and ecumenical tradition" (Lutheran Church of America, I.33), a "unity in faith, sacramental life, spiritual experience and witness to Christ" (Russian Orthodox Church, II.6), a "unity which

---

[42] Church of Ireland, I.63; Evangelical Church of the Lutheran Confession in Brazil, II.100; Estonian Evangelical Lutheran Church, IV.45; Evangelical Lutheran Church in Oldenburg, IV. 73-74; Presbyterian Church in Ireland, III.221; Evangelical Church of Kurhessen-Waldeck, V.95; Community of Disciples/Church of Christ in Zaire, VI.130; Burma Baptist Convention, IV.190; Moravian Church in Great Britain, III.284.

we Orthodox believe to be essentially preserved within the Orthodox Church despite our many sins and human divisions" (Orthodox Church in America, III.15), a unity which is a "dynamic conciliar fellowship in the pursuit of common goals informed by the Holy Spirit" (Armenian Apostolic Church, II.30). It is a unity which "is not an end in itself but for the service of God and the mission to the world" (Church of England, III.65), which "points to God's intention to unite the whole human race" (Scottish Episcopal Church, II.56). Some Lutheran churches indicate that they understand the goal of visible unity in terms of the concept of "unity in reconciled diversity" (Evangelical Lutheran Church in Bavaria, IV.40-41; Evangelical Church of the Augsburg Confession in Romania, IV.82; North Elbian Evangelical Lutheran Church, I.52, which quotes with approval the 1984 Budapest statement of the Lutheran World Federation on "The Unity We Seek").

36. Other responses express the goal of unity in their own words like, e.g., the Church of the Czech Brethren: "We understand this unity as a fellowship of Christians under the word and at the table of the Lord and as a missionary and diaconal ministry of the church" (IV.110). Several responses, especially from Free churches, question however the orientation of BEM towards visible unity.[43] "In our tradition unity has not been founded on baptism, eucharist and ministry, but on faith in Christ and on the fellowship of the Holy Spirit," says the Baptist Union of Denmark (III.247). In a similar way the priority of "spiritual unity" is emphasized by others,[44] and the so-called non-sacramental communions also affirm that "unity is a fellowship of the Spirit" (Religious Society of Friends in Great Britain, II.226) which "should and can most effectively be made visible (in) Christian witness and service" (Salvation Army, IV.233).

37. Several responses reflect on the methods and criteria underlying the search for unity. The Church of Norway stresses that unity must be founded on what is central and basic and that unity is not identical with uniformity. Because the themes treated in BEM are constitutive for the church they also form the basis for church unity (II.107). Making an explicit reference to the 1975 Nairobi statement on "conciliar fellowship", the Roman Catholic response regards baptism, eucharist and ministry as "some of the fundamental elements of a local church truly

---

[43] E.g. Evangelical Methodist Church in the German Democratic Republic, IV.168; Baptist Union of Scotland, III.232; Lutheran Church in America, II.88.

[44] E.g. Union of Evangelical Free Churches (Baptists) in the GDR, IV.191.

united" (VI.6). A major concern is expressed by the Church of Scotland: "We do not need consensus about everything... To achieve unity, churches must be agreed on that which is required and on no more than is sufficient" (I.90).[45] The United Reformed Church in the United Kingdom concludes from this: "We therefore believe that more attention needs to be given to the nature and extent of the agreement required for visible unity" (I.103). In this connection the Finnish Orthodox Church finds that BEM "supports freedom in matters which are not absolutely essential to the unity of the church" (II.25) and "Disciples applaud BEM's concept of 'unity with diversity' as a model for ecumenical growth" (Christian Church — Disciples of Christ in the USA, I.113). But the Baptist Union of Great Britain and Ireland, on the contrary, feels that the "model of visible unity assumed and the nature of consensus sought make inadequate allowance for a diversity which is arguably compatible with living in communion one with another" (I.77). The different positions on this issue clearly need further discussion and clarification, as does "our vision of the nature of the unity we should seek" (Armenian Apostolic Church, II.31).[46] Finally, the Anglican Church of the Southern Cone raises the question whether the common truth will be found in our union or whether Christians should unite on the basis of the truth (I.55-56), which is taken up by the Evangelical Lutheran Church of Finland with reference to the statement in the preface of BEM (p.ix) according to which full consensus will only be possible after the churches live and act together in unity. It regards as a mistaken interpretation that "common doctrine would only be a product of common experience" (III.127). This is again a point which requires further clarification.

38. The recently much discussed concept of "reception" belongs to the area of methodological considerations. Several responses comment on this concept. Their general orientation is expressed by the response of the Church of the Brethren (in the USA): "*Reception* refers to all phases of the process whereby a church appropriates the fruits of ecumenical conversation as integral to its own life and faith. It is a process that may take years and only comes to fruition by the power of the Holy Spirit. The purpose of the 'process of reception' is to renew all churches, and all

---

[45] For similar statements, cf. e.g. Evangelical Lutheran Church in Oldenburg, IV.75; American Baptist Churches in the USA, III.258 ("legitimate diversity").
[46] The same request is being made by the Baptist Union of Great Britain and Ireland, I.77; Anglican Church of Canada ("Organic unity? Federal structure with mutual recognition?"), II.46; United Reformed Church in the United Kingdom, I.108.

Christians, in faith, prayer and responsible witness in the world" (VI.105).[47] The United Methodist Church, USA, to add a similar view, says: "By 'reception' we understand the concept to mean the process by which the ideas of BEM are becoming a regular part of our church's worship, theology and life" (II.178).

11. Conclusion

39. The summaries of the churches' responses in the preceding parts, the indications of those churches which have directly responded to the questions of the preface to BEM ("the consequences your church can draw from this text for its relations and dialogues with other churches" and "the guidance your church can take from this text for its worship, educational, ethical and spiritual life and witness") and references to implications for the theology and practice of the churches when commenting on the three sections of BEM — all this provides ample evidence for the following conclusion. Most churches have not regarded the Lima document simply as a theological text to be reviewed within the framework and perspective of their own tradition and position. There seems to be a clear awareness that BEM is the result and an instrument of a broader and ongoing historical process in twentieth-century church history. And there is in most responses an explicit readiness expressed that, whatever the limitations of such a document might be, its content and purpose must be allowed to challenge one's own teaching and practice and to open it to the richness of the insights and experiences of other churches. *Baptism, Eucharist and Ministry* is thus seen as a significant result, expression and instrument of the movement towards that unity in faith, sacramental communion and common witness and service in the world to which the churches are called by their Lord and Saviour.

> Finally we would like to offer our prayer for the continuing reception of BEM. May God grant us penitence, humility and wisdom to learn from each other, and work together so that God's will may be done on earth, as it is done in heaven (Burma Baptist Convention, IV.186).

---

[47] Cf. also Evangelical Church of North West Germany, IV.93-94; Evangelical Church of Westphalia, IV.137; Episcopal Church, USA, II.59.

B. THE RESPONSES TO THE BAPTISM SECTION

1. Introduction

1. In general the responses of the churches to the section on baptism register gratitude for the work and affirm the impressive degree of agreement and convergence towards consensus. The text is "perhaps the best ecumenical statement that has been produced in portraying a very full meaning to the act";[1] "we believe that the baptism section of the Lima Text, firmly based as it is in Scripture, does witness to the faith of the church through the ages".[2] Several responses regard the section as the most satisfactory text of the three;[3] "looking at the three documents as a whole, we find this the most acceptable, and in general terms could be accepted by our congregations".[4] Many responses recognize the importance of the text's stress on baptism as the primary and fundamental sacrament of unity and the implications of this for the ecumenical endeavour. They approve the final sentence of paragraph 6: "therefore, our one baptism into Christ constitutes a call to the churches to overcome their divisions and visibly manifest their fellowship".[5]

2. There is one voice which, after pointing to what is believed to be "decisive weaknesses", concludes "we cannot approve the baptismal statement".[6] Others who affirm much in the text also question how far agreements stated are in fact substantial agreements or whether they mask underlying differences.[7] The Baptist Union of Great Britain, for example, asks whether there are not fundamental assumptions which need exposure and assessment while several other churches find the text in places ambiguous.[8] The Anglican Church of the Province of the Southern Cone fears that in such a multilateral text "each participant interprets the

---

[1] Christian Church (Disciples of Christ) in Canada, III.264.
[2] Church of England, III.41; cf. also Lutheran Church in America, I.35; Church of North India, II.70; Uniting Church in Australia, IV.155; Evangelical Lutheran Church in the Netherlands, V.19; Reformed Church in Hungary, V.162, etc.
[3] Episcopal Church USA, II.59; Evangelical Methodist Church: Central Conference in the Federal Republic of Germany and West Berlin, IV.173.
[4] Waldensian Evangelical Church of the River Plate (Uruguay), IV.119.
[5] Evangelical-Reformed Church of North-West Germany, IV.95; Evangelical Church of Kurhessen-Waldeck, V.66; Scottish Episcopal Church, II.52.
[6] Independent Evangelical Lutheran Church (Federal Republic of Germany and West Berlin), VI.54.
[7] American Lutheran Church, II.81-82.
[8] I.70ff.; American Lutheran Church, II.82.

documents from his own perspective" (I.54). And the Methodist Church of Great Britain highlights the difficulty that arises when it is possible to read a text in different ways so that apparently unreconcilable positions are heard (II.220).

3. Many of the responses reflect the particular history of a church and the special theological emphases that church has sought to safeguard. So the Lutheran responses seek to protect an emphasis on word alongside sacrament and emphasize baptism as the sacrament of justification; Baptist responses challenge the understanding of the text on the meaning of "re-baptism"; Orthodox responses guard the understanding of the gift of the Spirit in chrismation; churches in developing countries reflect more upon the cultural context of baptism; churches in Europe reflect on the challenge of so-called "indiscriminate baptism" in a post-Christian secularized society; and the experience of the united churches points to the enrichment of living with diversity in unity. However, it is by no means the case that churches from the same Christian World Communion make necessarily identical comments.[9]

4. It is mainly within an affirmation of achievement that churches refer to issues that need further work. This reflection of the Roman Catholic Church is typical of many: the text contains "much we can agree with, as well as points to be studied further in the Faith and Order process" (VI.16). In general there is welcome for the text's firm grounding in holy scripture; the recognition of a fundamental relation that exists between God's gift and the human response of faith; the insistence on the priority of God's initiative, the setting of the individual's response of faith within the context of the faith of the believing community; the emphasis upon initiation as a process; the stress on the ethical implications of baptism; and the relation between a common baptism and the imperative to witness to that in unity; and many, though not all, comment favourably on the warning against both "indiscriminate baptism" and what is called "re-baptism".[10]

2. The biblical basis of baptism (B.1 and 2)

5. The text begins with an understanding of baptism set forth in the holy scripture. Almost all the responses applaud this biblical grounding which summarizes the New Testament view of baptism administered in

---

[9] This can be seen in the collation of responses of the Provinces of the Anglican Communion to *The Emmaus Report*, ACC, 1987.

[10] Church of England, III.41ff.

water in the name of the Father, Son and Holy Spirit, as being a participation in Christ's death and resurrection, a washing away of sin, a new birth, an enlightenment by Christ, a re-clothing in Christ, a renewal by the Spirit, a liberation into a new humanity, an act of justification, God's gift of the anointing and the promise of the Holy Spirit, a sign and seal of common discipleship and therefore a basic bond of Christian unity. A few responses, however, suggest an inadequacy of biblical presentation. This is particularly noted in respect of baptism and the biblical notion of covenant with its deep roots in the Old Testament. The text is thought not to do justice to the idea of baptism as entry into the new covenant, according to one response, as analogous to circumcision as the entry into the old covenant.[11]

6. Whereas the Salvation Army and the Quakers question whether the practice of baptism was in fact universal from the beginning[12] — as does the Church of North India (II.71) — others believe that the text does not do enough justice to the biblical witness to the practice of infant baptism.[13] The Evangelical Lutheran Church in Württemberg suggests "examining anew whether infant baptism has not been as much practised in New Testament times (B.11) as the baptism of adults".[14] On the other hand the Roman Catholic Church sees the constant practice of the church as sufficient justification for the practice of infant baptism (VI.13). And the Romanian Orthodox Church makes the point that the text should "study thoroughly infant baptism as current practice of the church as early as the apostolic age" (III.6).

3. The meaning of baptism (B.2-7)

7. Paragraphs 2-7 of the text present the rich meaning of baptism, in its manifold perspectives. Most of the churches have accepted the general comments in this section on the meaning of baptism. However a number of churches detect a certain ambiguity in the text. What is implied in the text's understanding of "baptism *is*"? Is it purely descriptive of a particu-

---

[11] Anglican Church of the Southern Cone, I.58; Evangelical Lutheran Church in Canada, II.103; Reformed Church in America, II.142; Presbyterian Church of USA, III.193; Union of Welsh Independents, III.269; Evangelical Lutheran Church of Iceland, IV.59; etc.

[12] The Salvation Army, IV.230; Religious Society of Friends (Quakers) in Great Britain, IV.220.

[13] Church of Sweden, II.127.

[14] V.4-25; cf. also Church in Wales, III.89; Evangelical Church of Kurhessen-Waldeck, V.98; Roman Catholic Church, VI.13, etc.

lar ritual action? Or does it carry with it essential meaning of what that rite effects? Two corresponding concerns lie behind these questions. The first is to know whether it is meant that the rite "effects" or that it "signifies" the elements of the Christian life into which the baptized person is initiated.[15] In other words, what is the relation between the sign and what is signified? Is baptism instrumental as a means by which something is to happen? The other concern relates to the notion that the text makes baptism itself the subject of the action: "baptism makes", "constitutes", "initiates", "gives", "has", "anticipates". Not a few responses claim that the language of the text goes too far in the direction of a mechanical understanding of baptism, suggesting "efficacious power" which — some fear — tends towards a "magical view of the sacrament".[16]

8. Though they do not wish to deny the efficacy of the sacrament of baptism, some responses ask for a clearer statement that it depends entirely on the gracious, free gift of God and not upon any "supposed automation in the rite". It is God alone who is truly acting in and through baptism. And it is God who gives the grace of salvation, a gift that can only be received. Reformation churches as well as Free churches stress clearly their conviction that the efficacy of baptism does not work *ex opere operato*, i.e., does not lie in the ritual action as such.[17] Nor does it depend upon any worth or merit of the recipient or celebrant, a point on which some Orthodox responses look for assurance in the text. The wish to clarify and make more precise the understanding of sacraments as implied in the text is shared by several churches.[18] The Methodist Church of Great Britain feels that the danger to understand the text "in terms of a mechanical process" could be avoided if images and formulations were not only related to "the baptismal moment, particularly the infant baptismal moment" but "to Christian life as a whole" (II.20). Concerning the issues mentioned here in paragraphs 7 and 8, see "Clarifications", A.6 and 7, and "Major Issues", B. Sacrament and Sacramentality.

9. A number of churches miss in the document more explicit references to sin or to the doctrine of original sin, though in B.2-4 sin is mentioned

---

[15] Baptist Union of Great Britain and Ireland, I.70; Methodist Church of Southern Africa, II.237-238.

[16] Church of North India, II.70f.; Swiss Protestant Church Federation, VI.80; American Lutheran Church, II.81.

[17] Presbyterian Church of Ireland, III.208; Evangelical Lutheran Church of France, III.161; United German Mennonite Congregations, VI.126; Baptist Union of Scotland, III.234.

[18] United Reformed Church in the United Kingdom, I.103; Baptist Union of Scotland, III.235.

several times. Lutheran churches in general wish more attention to be given to the context of sin and grace which is crucial for the understanding of baptism. "The text does not articulate an adequate understanding of the dynamic of sin and grace," says the American Lutheran Church (II.81), and the Church of Norway claims the characteristic Lutheran understanding of the baptized as being "righteous and sinner at the same time".[19] The Roman Catholic Church points to the "necessity of baptism for salvation" by relating the universality of human sinfulness, expressed in the doctrine of original sin, to the "universal need for salvation" and to Jesus Christ as the "universal Saviour" (VI.12). The Evangelical Church of the Augsburg Confession of Alsace and Lorraine regrets, in the same context, "the absence of any development of the relationship between baptism and penitence as an actualisation of baptism" (III.149f.). This point is further discussed in "Clarifications", A.8 and 9.

10. The paragraphs which explore the meaning of baptism hint at the new life in Christ which entails ethical consequences implied in the New Testament. The Church of the Brethren in the United States of America observes that there is a predominance in the text of baptismal images of dying over images of rising into new life in Christ (VI.109). Many responses regret that those ethical consequences were not treated more explicitly: "we would have welcomed a more explicit treatment of the relation of baptism to the life of faithfulness in the world";[20] "it is necessary to elaborate the question of the newness of one's human character after baptism, the relationship of baptism to one's membership in the kingdom of God and the reflection of this fact in one's new ethical orientation".[21] The National Council of Churches in Korea believes that "the important aspect of being called into the discipleship of Jesus Christ seems to have been weakened... But from the experience of the third-world Christian experience, it is a concrete and living response to the call of God to participate in the struggle of history and situation of the world".[22] The Evangelical Presbyterian Church in Ghana writes: "There

---

[19] II.112; see also Lutheran Church in Hungary, III.129; Lutheran Church — Missouri Synod, III.135; Evangelical Lutheran Church in Bavaria, IV.29; Lutheran Church in America, I.34; Church of Sweden, II.127; Reformed Church of Alsace and Lorraine, III.166; Methodist Church in Ireland, II.230f.

[20] United Church of Canada, II.277; Lutheran Church in Hungary, III.129.

[21] Czechoslovak Hussite Church, II.302.

[22] VI.136; cf. also The Episcopal Church of the USA, II.59; The Lutheran Church of Australia, II.88; Church of the Brethren USA, VI.109; United German Mennonite Congregations, VI.126; The Evangelical Presbyterian Church in Ghana, VI.89; etc.

is no magical secret in baptism. What is secret in it is the change from the good life to a better life which gradually evolves from a person. It is what we call *ahbeyeyenono*, a new way of living, that is essential" (VI.89). Several churches would like to have seen more emphasis put on the "missiological" implications of baptism.[23]

4. Baptism and faith (B.8-10)

11. "Baptism is both God's gift and our human response to that gift" (B.8). Very many responses comment upon the question of the relation of God's gift and the human response of faith. The Roman Catholic Church recognizes that "there is a deep doctrine of grace inherent in the explanation given in 8-10 of how human response meets the gift of God in baptism. The text is an invitation to a deep baptismal spirituality" (VI.13). Many responses believe that the necessary inter-relation between divine initiative and human response as expressed in the scriptures has been maintained both in these paragraphs and throughout the entire text. "In spite of the difficulty of maintaining this delicate balance in such a closely argued text, we believe that as a whole the text does achieve this. At the same time it is faithful to the stress on the prior gift of God in implanting new life and incorporating the baptized person into the already existing fellowship of the Spirit... While the renunciation, the profession of faith and the vows are essential parts of the response of the believer, the prime initiative is understood to lie with the grace of God rather than with the decision of men and women."[24]

12. Not all the responses agree with this estimate of the matter. There are those, including the American Lutheran Church, the United Reformed Church in the United Kingdom, the North Elbian Lutheran Church and the Lutheran Church of Australia who maintain that baptism as a rite of commitment is overemphasized, placing too much upon the human response and not on God's act of grace. Among others the Church of Norway states that baptism is first an action of God, an objective gift: this is not expressed loudly enough in the text with the consequence that baptism becomes too subjective. Baptism is a gift and faith itself is part of the gift of God; that gift is dependent upon Christ offered in the sacrament (II.111f.). For further comments on the issue of baptism and faith see "Clarifications", A.2.

---

[23] United Church of Christ in Japan, II.288; Mar Thoma Syrian Church of Malabar, IV.8; Federation of the Evangelical Churches in the GDR, V.127.
[24] Church of England, III.34; Evangelical Lutheran Church of Denmark, IV.109.

13. It is not only the relation between God's gift of grace and human response that some churches take issue with but the very understanding of grace itself. For example, the Methodist Church of New Zealand asks for more work on a theology of grace (I.80). Is baptismal grace from the Father, or the Son or the Holy Spirit? What is the relation of the activity of the three persons of the Holy Trinity in baptism? If the text aims at an underlying Trinitarian approach the responses do not always recognize that. Some also ask for a clearer presentation of the relation or distinction between God's act of justification in baptism and the Holy Spirit's work of sanctification in the life of the baptized.[25] The Roman Catholic Church's response suggests that there is too little emphasis upon the ecclesiological dimension of baptismal grace. "The references to the church in these paragraphs, and particularly the use of the word 'context' to describe its role (B.10), seem, however, less than adequate to express the ecclesiological dimension of baptismal grace."[26]

14. If the particular understanding of grace that the text works with is not clear to some, neither is the understanding of faith. Is faith to do with intellectual assent to propositions or more to do with an attitude of trust and confidence and what is implied about Christian assurance in the sacrament of baptism? The Church of Norway has this to say about "faith" in the text: "From our understanding, it is unclear if the BEM text in fact puts too much stress on faith as a function of human consciousness and consequently is in danger of operating with a psychological concept of faith... we in our tradition understand faith to be a gift of God which is given and created through the administration of grace" (II.111).

5. Baptism of believers and infants (B.11-13)

15. The balance held in the text between God's gracious gift and the human response of faith, the emphasis upon baptism as a decisive beginning of an initiatory process, and the importance of the community of faith as the context for the individual's act of faith and growth in faith are welcomed as appropriate bases by many for holding together the two practices of what the text calls baptism of believers and baptism of infants. Many of the responses welcome an emerging agreement between

---

[25] Evangelical Methodist Church: Central Conference in the German Democratic Republic, IV.169; Presbyterian Church in Ireland, III.207-208.
[26] VI.13; see also the Ecumenical Patriarchate of Constantinople, IV.4f.

those who can now accept the two practices as "equivalent alternatives".[27] And some of the united churches testify from their experience to the enrichment of living in a church with the two practices.[28]

16. While affirming the diversity of baptismal practices, a number of responses point out that the terminology used in the text of "infant baptism" contrasted with "believer's baptism" is unhelpful and, in fact, inaccurate.[29] Infant baptism ought rather to be set side by side with the baptism of those able to make a personal testimony of faith. For infant baptism is within the context of the believing community and can, therefore, rightly be said to be "believer's baptism". See also "Clarifications", A.3.

17. There are those, however, who challenge the text for not simply holding together two baptismal practices but for going beyond this to suggest that adult believer's baptism is the norm from the New Testament model and that infant baptism should be understood only within this norm. Whatever the base in New Testament times they want to underline the practice of infant baptism as acceptable as a genuinely authentic alternative, witnessing to the primacy of God's gift of grace which is not dependent upon the explicit faith response of the individual.[30]

18. On the other hand, particularly Baptist churches are not happy with the way in which the text holds the two baptismal practices together. The text has too easily settled for compromise and too easily dismissed a fundamental incompatibility between infant and adult believer's baptism. They detect a theological difficulty in maintaining one baptism in two different forms. The Baptist Union of Denmark speaks for many: "We appreciate the statement of the text that 'baptism upon personal profession of faith is the most clearly attested pattern in the New Testament documents'. Although 'the possibility that infant baptism was also practised in the apostolic age cannot be excluded', serious problems arise still for many Baptists when the document applies the indeed excellent theology on baptism (1-10) equally to both modes of baptism and calls them 'equivalent alternatives'. To our minds there are still theological difficulties involved in maintaining that the church has one baptism in two different forms that are on the same level. Underlining the difficulty we

---

[27] Russian Orthodox Church, II.7; Evangelical Lutheran Church of Denmark, III.109; Evangelical Lutheran Church of Finland, III.119; etc.
[28] United Reformed Church in the United Kingdom, I.102.
[29] Evangelical Church of Westphalia, IV.144.
[30] Church in Wales, III.89; Evangelical Lutheran Church of Finland, III.119.

frankly admit the greatest challenge to us is precisely here. However, the treatment of the problem by the document is not convincing to us" (III.248).[31]

19. A special question related to baptism of those able to make a response for themselves is raised in the concern for baptism of the handicapped. Under the heading of "cognition and persons with handicapping conditions" the United Methodist Church of the USA comments that "the ongoing debate over the relation of divine grace and human response in baptism usually pits 'infants' against 'adults'; but this is deceptive, for it leaves out a great number of people who are not so helpless as infants, but who lack sufficient intellectual capacity to make a mature profession of faith. Just as Jesus gave special attention to the children and adults with severe handicapping conditions, so the church today should be able, on sound theological and psychological grounds, to provide the blessing of baptism and life in the community for persons who are physically and mentally impaired" (II.187). A similar concern is expressed by the United Church of Christ in Japan (II.289).

20. The Church of England comments that "the ecumenical duty of listening to and learning from each other is placed by the text on both those who practise infant baptism and those who practise 'believer's baptism' alike. The text does not ask Baptists, or anyone else, to cease from deferring baptism either until adult life, or at least until conscious choice is possible, nor to accept the practice of infant baptism as the standing pattern. Rather it asks those who practise only 'believer's baptism' to acknowledge that in those communions where, by very ancient tradition indeed, infants are admitted to the sacrament, those candidates are validly and effectively received into the church of Christ and are made children of God, members of Christ, and inheritors of the kingdom of heaven" (III.34). The Federation of the Evangelical Churches in the GDR therefore expresses the hope that churches which agree on the Lima text in this respect "will recognize our baptizing of children and infants as true baptism". They feel that the text should have made a better distinction between the different "forms of baptismal practices" rather than giving the impression that different "kinds" of baptism existed (V.125,148).

21. A great many responses affirm the text's insistence that baptism is unrepeatable. Some plead, however, for a much clearer theology for such a view.[32] The Methodist Church of New Zealand says that the "bold

---

[31] Cf. Baptist Union of Scotland, III.235; Baptist Union of Sweden, IV.201.
[32] Church of North India, II.71; Church of South India, II.75; etc.

statement of unrepeatability" is insufficient: it needs to be argued for (I.80). The Church of North India asks: How can one repeat the unrepeatable and the Presbyterian Church of Canada: How can this be for those who do not see infant baptism as baptism.[33] A number of responses suggest the issue needs deeper treatment.[34] There are those who point out the hurt they feel when others, including churches of both the Catholic and Protestant persuasion, do in fact conduct what they regard as second baptism.[35]

22. The text uses the phrase "any practice which might be interpreted as re-baptism should be avoided". The Baptist Union of Great Britain and Ireland sees this as "unacceptable in the present form since, on some interpretations, nothing could pass through so restrictive a sieve. In cases of infant baptism which are neither accompanied nor followed by any of the significant features of the initiating process to which the report amply draws attention, and where the individual involved is convinced out of an instructed conscience that Christian obedience requires believer's baptism, we cannot agree that an *a priori* universal bar should operate" (I.71). The Evangelical Lutheran Church of Finland sums up the problem in this way: "From the point of view of interchurch fellowship baptism is an unsolved problem, for the reason that most churches which reject infant baptism do not regard the baptism of adults who have been baptised as infants as re-baptism" (III.120).

6. Baptism — chrismation — confirmation (B.14-15)

23. There is in the text a strong emphasis upon baptism as a decisive "beginning" in a process: "Baptism is related not only to momentary experience, but to life-long growth into Christ" (B.9). Many churches welcome this emphasis on initiation as a process for it provides for all the necessary elements — including responsible faith commitment — to find a place.[36] Some, however, fear that it is precisely at this point that the text conceals ambiguity. It sometimes uses the term "baptism" when what is referred to seems to be the total initiation process rather than the first event *within* a total process: "the statements that may be defensible where and if 'baptism' is a shorthand term for total initiation become suspect

---

[33] II.71; Presbyterian Church of Canada, II.154.
[34] Episcopal Church USA, II.59; Church of Norway, II.110; Evangelical Church in Rhineland (FRG), V.73.
[35] Anglican Church of the Southern Cone, I.57.
[36] Church of England, III.35.

when applied *simpliciter* to the baptismal rite as administered to infants".[37]

24. A number of responses express disappointment at the lack of clarity in the text on either the meaning of, or the relation between, the various parts of the initiation process — baptism, chrismation, confirmation, admission to holy communion. For example the Romanian Orthodox Church suggests that the document should "state clearly the relation between baptism, chrismation and the eucharist which are constitutive of the Christian initiation..."[38] The Church of England suggests that this lack of clarity is not surprising for scripture and the earliest Tradition allow for the possibility of more than one answer and a diversity of opinion is reflected in the life and practice both within and between denominations (III.38).

25. Paragraph 14 of the text refers to the diversity of opinion that exists on the gift of the Spirit in the initiation process (baptism, chrismation, confirmation). This diversity is confirmed in the responses of the churches. While not denying that the Holy Spirit is active in baptism most Orthodox responses make a distinction between baptismal and paschal dying and rising in Christ which unites us with Christ, and chrismation as the pentecostal sealing with the gift of the Holy Spirit itself. Like the Orthodox Church in America they ask for chrismation to be clearly defined (III.16). Some Anglican responses affirm the rite of chrismation, sometimes as part of the rite of baptism, sometimes as joined with confirmation, and see it as an appropriate sign of the gift of the Holy Spirit. At the same time they are clear that the gift of the Holy Spirit in baptism as the initial rite of the initiation process is an essential part of the faith of the church through the ages. The Roman Catholic response states that "the emergence of a distinctive sacramental rite called chrismation or confirmation is a normative development in the faith of the church. While the gift of the Holy Spirit is given in baptism, certain aspects of that pentecostal gift have come to be effectively symbolized in the liturgy of Christian initiation by anointing with perfumed oil and a prayer with laying on of hands." It therefore believes "that chrismation/confirmation is a sacrament distinct from baptism in which there is given a special and unique gift of the Holy Spirit" (VI.15). The Church of England makes the additional point that episcopal confirmation *effectively* signifies the candidate is a member of the universal church in which the bishop is a visible

---
[37] Baptist Union of Great Britain and Ireland, I.71.
[38] III.6; see also Malankara Orthodox Syrian Church (India), V.4.

sign of continuity (III.39). The United Protestant Church of Belgium however sees "serious problems" when baptism and confirmation are dissociated and confirmation is "regarded as a sacramental act conferring the 'fullness of the Holy Spirit and completing baptism'" (III.169). On this issue see also "Clarifications", A.10.

26. In many churches there is generally perplexity over the rite of confirmation and its relation to baptism. This is reflected in the comment of the Church of the Province of New Zealand. "Within the Anglican Church there is a growing challenge to the classic Anglican pattern of interposing a separate rite of confirmation between baptism and participation in the eucharist."[39] Some see confirmation primarily as an occasion when Christians renew the acts of repentance and faith made in their name (or which they make at baptism), an occasion for blessing and, in some senses, an occasion of grace; others see it as a second sacramental act linked to baptism which effects a further work of the Holy Spirit; others see it as the sacramental act by which the Spirit is given.

27. The emphasis on initiation as a process raises the question of the relation between baptism, confirmation and first communion. Many of the responses stress that it is baptism that is the entrance to eucharistic living; in each eucharist baptism is reaffirmed and the Christian confirmed in a life of grace.[40] Even some of those churches which stress the importance and the sacramental nature of confirmation move in the direction of encouraging children's communion before confirmation. The Church of the Province of New Zealand mentions the challenge to the classic Anglican pattern of excluding baptized children from the eucharist. It maintains two practices: "admission to holy communion after episcopal confirmation, and admission of children to holy communion after due preparation but before confirmation" (II.65). It appears that today many Reformation and Free churches in Europe and North America view confirmation less and less as strictly the way to holy communion. See also "Clarifications", A.5.

28. Generally responses affirm the need expressed in BEM for much more serious catechetical work both with those to be baptized and with godparents.[41] Many stress the need for regular reaffirmation of baptismal

---

[39] II.65; Church in Wales, III.89; see Church of the Province of Southern Africa, III.101.

[40] There is however one response that raises the question whether even baptism itself should be required for admittance to the eucharist: Theological Committee of the National Council of Churches in Korea, VI.136.

[41] Swiss Protestant Church Federation, VI.8; Roman Catholic Church, VI.14.

vows, not only in confirmation and in the regular celebration of the eucharist but in the practice of confession and absolution, both private and public or in the Easter vigil or in a service like the Methodist covenant service.

29. A number of responses welcome services of thanksgiving for the life of a child and blessing of infants prior to the administration of baptism.[42] The Evangelical Church in Berlin Brandenburg sums the situation up for many when it writes: "We too feel the need 'to express more visibly the fact that children are placed under the protection of God's grace', and some ministers and members are thinking about the presentation and blessing of infants or children in an act of worship prior to the administration of baptism" (VI.60). However several other churches express their hesitation to accept a special rite of blessing for those children, for they fear that this would weaken the completeness and integrity of the meaning of the sacrament of baptism.[43]

7. Towards mutual recognition of baptism (B.15-16)

30. Most responses affirm the text's insistence that baptism is a basic bond of unity.[44] The churches of the Reformed tradition in the Netherlands believe that "those churches which recognize the faith of the church in this (i.e. the baptism section) can acknowledge the baptism of the other and so the baptismal community can be restored and/or supported".[45] The United Reformed Church points to the importance of already having a common baptismal certificate for churches in Great Britain.[46] The Church of England suggests that this implies both some recognition of ecclesial reality and that some would even argue that such mutual recognition of baptism also implies a certain degree of ministerial acknowledgment (III.37). In the same line the Anglican Church of Canada holds that once baptism is recognized, we must be prepared to deal with the obvious consequences, namely full communion and mutual recognition of ordained ministry (II.40).

31. All churches responding to BEM agree that baptism is "incorporation into the body of Christ". Almost all are ready to recognize some

---

[42] Baptist Union of Scotland, III.235; United Mennonite Congregations, VI.126; etc.
[43] Evangelical Church in Hessen and Nassau, IV.132; United Church of Christ in Japan, II.288.
[44] Church of Scotland (Reformed,) I.90; Christian Church (Disciples of Christ), I.115; Evangelical Church of Rhineland, V.74.
[45] Netherlands Reformed Church/Reformed Churches in the Netherlands, IV.105.
[46] I.106; see Scottish Episcopal Church, II.52.

baptisms outside their institutional boundaries as being incorporation into this body which is the church. They do so even when they are unable to recognize the full ecclesial reality of the churches in which these baptisms occur. This raises important questions about the nature of the church in relation to baptism, a point specifically raised in several responses. For example, the response of the Roman Catholic Church: "The document does not here give adequate attention, however, to the implications of the fact that a person is baptized within a particular fellowship in a divided Christianity... It draws attention to the contradiction between one baptism and divided Christian communities, and calls for an overcoming of division and a visible manifestation of baptismal fellowship" (VI.11). The Orthodox Church in America similarly says that "the 'body of Christ' into which we are initiated in baptism is the church.... Throughout our participation in the ecumenical movement, we Orthodox have affirmed that the Orthodox Church is indeed the one body of Christ, and we firmly believe that the new birth of the faithful in baptism leads to this one church. Herein, we are convinced, lies the significance of the Orthodox Church's continuing practice, authorized by the ecumenical councils, of receiving as already baptized those coming to her from certain groups, while insisting upon baptism for those coming from other groups whose baptism she is unable to recognize" (III.17). What is required here, as this response specifically invites, is an explanation of "the implications of this practice [i.e., the recognition of authentic and acceptable baptisms in divided churches] for the unity of Christians in the one church of Christ"; and, further, a clarification of what is implied about the ecclesial reality of those communities in which these baptisms, so recognized, are performed. For indeed, the "implications" of this recognition are at the very heart of the churches' self-understanding in their search for visible unity.

8. Celebration of baptism (B.17-23)

32. The Roman Catholic Church's response finds this part of the text is "liturgically rich" and includes all the "classical elements" (VI.15). An acceptance of what is said would, the response notes, contribute greatly towards mutual recognition of baptism. But there are questions raised by some responses: some churches have been made to revalue the symbolism of immersion together with pouring or sprinkling with water;[47] others raise the question of gender-free language of the Trinitarian formula;[48]

---

[47] Presbyterian Church (USA), III.194.
[48] Anglican Church of Canada, II.45.

others question private baptisms. The Orthodox Church in America asks about the creed used in baptism: "For the Orthodox, the content of the credal confession of faith made at baptism is of crucial importance" (III.16).

9. Apparently "indiscriminate" baptism (B.23)

33. Many responses register gratitude for the text's warning against "indiscriminate baptism". Anglicans and larger European Reformation churches in particular respond to this warmly. But the Scottish Episcopal Church indicates that it is a delicate matter to judge who should be baptized and who deferred as none of our responses to God's continual offering of his grace is without ambiguity and imperfection. There is, however, a problem when baptism becomes a badge of social acceptance rather than the willing acceptance of a new orientation in life and a relationship with God.[49]

10. Cultural challenges

34. It is the churches from Africa and Asia which point particularly to contextual challenges in baptism. The Church of South India mentions that in India some feel that repetition of baptism or re-baptism is not contrary to the Indian religious practice of dipping in sacred rivers. In the present situation in India baptism is a great disadvantage to the poorer sections of the community. Privileges are given to the scheduled castes and scheduled tribes and privileges stop as soon as a person becomes a Christian. The Church of South India is not the only church to mention the damaging custom of taking a Christian name which is foreign to the country, suggesting that baptism somehow implies moving from one culture to another (II.74). The Presbyterian Church of Rwanda mentions the danger of certain gestures in the baptismal rite which can be construed as magical (III.183). The Melanesian Council of Churches points out that the community in Melanesia always includes the recent dead, the Spirit and ancestors. The baptism text makes no mention of incorporation into this wider community (V.180f.).

11. Communities who do not practise water baptism

35. The reflections of the Quakers on the baptism text have to be held within the framework of the assertion that "however valid and vital outward sacraments are for others, they are not, in our experience,

---

[49] II.53; see Church of Norway, II.109.

necessary for the operation of God's grace... The whole of our everyday experience is the stuff of our religious awareness, it is here that God is best known to us."[50] The Quaker understanding of baptism "is that it is not a single act of initiation but a continuing growth in the Holy Spirit and a commitment which must be continually renewed". This life-long commitment, continually renewed, leads to a rejection of water baptism for it has no necessary connection between the single event and the experience of transformation by the Spirit. "We cannot see that this rite should be used as the only way of becoming a member of the body of Christ. Nor do we find the use of water baptism to be an inescapable inference from the New Testament's account of Jesus' life and practice."[51]

36. The Salvation Army's response to the Lima text is set within the overall comment that the Army's traditional approach to the subjects dealt with differs significantly from the hypothesis on which the present study rests. About baptism they say "the only distinctive and utterly unique Christian baptism is baptism with the Holy Spirit". Further, much of what is claimed for baptism can be similarly claimed for Christians who are not baptized with water. The Salvation Army regrets that more was not said about "baptism of the Holy Spirit without water" (see commentary to B.21c) (IV.236 and 241).

37. Both the responses of the Quakers and of the Salvation Army welcome the challenge of the Lima text which makes them examine their own theological position vis-à-vis baptism, eucharist and ministry. And in spite of fundamental differences, they recognize questions which are shared by them with many other churches including the appropriate age for church membership, the place of the child within the family of the church and the need for more effective Christian nurture.

Conclusion

38. The most remarkable fact emerging from the responses of churches to the baptism section is the degree of convergence that exists in areas of previous dissension, and the willingness of the churches, in the face of continuing differences, to seek together a common language and understanding. The encouragement to pursue this work for the sake of the visible unity of the church, a unity grounded in baptism, is heartening.

---

[50] Religious Society of Friends (Quakers) in Great Britain, IV.218f.
[51] Religious Society of Friends (Quakers) in Great Britain, IV.219f.; cf. also Quakers of the Netherlands, III.297, and Canadian Yearly Meeting of the Religious Society of Friends, III.300.

The reality of the remaining differences cannot be overlooked. These do not only concern different understandings of baptism as such, but also reflect different conceptions of faith, the action of the Holy Spirit, the church, membership of the church and the Christian life itself. It is crucially important therefore that the facing of the remaining differences should be related to fresh thinking on the areas highlighted in chapter V. Understanding of these areas — such as ecclesiology, sacramentality, and the sources of Christian authority in scripture, Tradition and traditions — will both influence, and be influenced by, our understandings of baptism. Recognition of this mutual interplay will ensure the integrity of the search for a deepening of the agreement which is sufficient and required for the unity of the church.

C. THE RESPONSES TO THE EUCHARIST SECTION

1. Reactions to main areas and directions of the text

1. The section on the eucharist has been regarded by several responses as the most satisfactory of the three parts of the Lima text: "This is the best section of BEM and the richest in content" (United Church of Christ in Japan, II.289).[1] It is praised for its "biblical spirit" (Bulgarian Orthodox Church, II.17)[2] and its "harmony with the teaching and witness of the early Church" (Finnish Orthodox Church, II.27).[3] "Drawing its inspiration from recent biblical, patristic and liturgical scholarship, it is eirenic in approach and successfully transcends the old divisive controversies" (Church of Ireland [Anglican], I.65). "If all the churches and ecclesial communities are able to accept at least the theological understanding and description of the celebration of the eucharist as described in BEM and implement it as part of their normal life, we believe that this would be an important development, and that these divided Christians

---

[1] Cf. Scottish Episcopal Church (II.49: "... represents a devotional and doctrinal consensus deeper and wider than the first and third parts"); United Methodist Church, Central and Southern Europe (II.204: "The section on communion appears to us to be the most well-balanced"); Presbyterian Church of New Zealand (II.175: "We found this a generous and far-sighted document with greater common ground than might have been expected").

[2] Cf. Anglican Church of Canada, II.39; Evangelical Church of the River Plate, Argentina, V.176; Evangelical-Reformed Church of North West Germany, IV.95.

[3] Cf. Bulgarian Orthodox Church, II.17; Roman Catholic Church, VI.16.

now stood on a new level in regard to achieving common faith on the eucharist" (Roman Catholic Church, VI.38).[4]

2. Practically unanimous approval is shown for the Trinitarian approach to the eucharist, summarized in E.14: "It is the Father who is the primary origin and final fulfilment of the eucharistic event. The incarnate Son of God by and in whom it is accomplished is its living centre. The Holy Spirit is the immeasurable strength of love which makes it possible and continues to make it effective."[5] Extensive also is the approval of the recognition given in the Lima text to the eucharist's redemptive purpose, cosmic range, and eschatological scope: it "sets the celebration of the meal firmly within the total action of God in creation, reconciliation and consummation" (Evangelical Church of the Augsburg Confession in Romania, IV.85).[6]

3. Within this general doctrinal framework, so positively accepted, the responses of the churches register progress on certain historically controversial issues. Most importantly, there is a very widespread willingness to agree in the confession of "Christ's real, living and active presence", as affirmed in the Lima text (E.13).[7] Some of these responses explicitly

---

[4] A small number of churches find a fundamental dissonance between the Lima document and their respective understandings of the Lord's supper, which they believe to be biblically grounded: Anglican Church of the Southern Cone, I.58f.; Presbyterian Church in Ireland, III.210-214; Presbyterian Church of Rwanda, III.183f.; Baptist Union of Scotland, III.236-239; Union of Welsh Independents, II.271.

[5] For example: Roman Catholic Church, VI.16,22; the Orthodox Church in America, III.18; the Mar Thoma Syrian Church of Malabar, IV.8f.; the Church of England, III.42,45; many Lutheran and United churches; Reformed Church of North-West Germany, IV.95; Presbyterian Church in Ireland, III.210; United Methodist Church, USA, II.188; Uniting Church in Australia, IV.158; Mission Covenant Church of Sweden, II.318; Baptist Union of Sweden, IV.205.

[6] Cf. e.g. Church of Sweden, II.131; Mar Thoma Syrian Church of Malabar, IV.9; Orthodox Church in America, III.18; United Church of Canada, (II.279: "We appreciate, particularly, the manner in which the text points to the rootedness of the eucharist in creation and the inclusion of the whole world in the eucharistic celebration"); United Protestant Church of Belgium, III.173; Evangelical Church of the Rhineland (V.82: "As Christ associates his presence with the signs of bread and wine which are elements of creation, so the whole of creation is included in the event of the Lord's supper"). For appreciation of the eschatological dimension of the eucharist, see below paragraphs 33-35.

[7] Roman Catholic Church, VI.21; Mar Thoma Church, IV.9; many Lutheran churches (American Lutheran Church, II.82; Lutheran Church in America, I.36; Finland, III.120; Iceland, IV.62; North Elbia, I.44; Norway, II.113; Romania, IV:86; Württemberg, V.26); Church of England, III.45f.; Church in Wales, II.84; Scottish Episcopal Church, II.49; Church of Scotland, I.86,89; United Reformed Church in the United Kingdom, I.104; Evangelical Churches of Baden, V.41f., Lippe, VI.70, and the River Plate, Argentina,

affirm that remaining differences "can be accommodated within the convergence formulated in the text" (cf. E.13, comm.). Others, just as explicitly, join those churches which still call — from various angles — for more precision in the account to be given of the presence.[8] Again, there is broad agreement that the Lord's supper includes a moment of eucharistic response on the part of the church to God's saving gift,[9] even though the notions of "offering" and "sacrifice" are still regarded as needing further clarification.[10] These matters, which are linked also to the technical terms of "anamnesis" and "epiklesis", will here be treated according to the sequence of the Lima text itself, see below, paragraphs 13-30, and "Clarifications", B.4-6.

V.177; the Swiss Protestant Church Federation, VI.82, and the Federation of Evangelical Churches in the GDR, V:134; several Methodist churches (United Methodist Church, USA, II.188; Central and Southern Europe, II.205; FRG, IV.177); United Church of Christ, USA, II.329; Church of North India, II.72; cf. Baptist Union of Sweden (IV.205: "The old crucial question of *how* Christ is present in the eucharist is answered in such a wise and cautious way").

[8] Among the Orthodox, the Bulgarian, II.18, the Romanian, III.8, the Russian, II.8; among the Lutherans, Bavaria, IV.33, Brunswick, VI.47, North Elbia, I.45, Norway, II.115, Romania, IV.88; among the Anglicans, Australia, (II.34: "The Anglican tradition has encompassed the views of those who see Christ's presence as being specifically linked with the elements and those who see Christ's presence as being found in the faithful reception of those elements. This latter viewpoint does not appear to find expression in the E section of BEM, save, possibly, in E.15 and commentary"), Canada, II.39, and the USA, II.60; among the Reformed, the Presbyterian Church in Canada, II.155f., in Ireland, II.213f., and the Church of Scotland, I.95; also Evangelical Church of the Rhineland, V.79, Church of South India, II.77, the Uniting Church in Australia, IV.158f., Old Catholic Church of Switzerland, V.11, and Roman Catholic Church, VI.21-23. For some Lutherans, suspicion about the realism of Lima's confession of Christ's presence is aroused by the failure to mention the *manducatio impiorum* (Lutheran Church in Australia, II.91; Lutheran Church Missouri Synod, III.137; Independent Evangelical Lutheran Church FRG, VI.55). On the presence of Christ, and particularly its "unique" mode in the eucharist (E.13), see further below, paragraphs 15-20.

[9] For example, the Lutheran Churches in Denmark, III.111, Finland, III.121f., France, III.150, and Württemberg, V.26; Reformed Church in America, II.146; Presbyterian Church of Wales, II.171; the Evangelical Churches in Baden, V.43f., Berlin-Brandenburg, VI.61f. and Kurhessen-Waldeck, V.96; the (Anglican) Church in Wales, III.83; the Methodist Church of Great Britain, III.222; Seventh Day Adventists, II.342.

[10] For example among the Lutherans, Missouri Synod, III.136, the Netherlands, V.20, Oldenburg, IV.76f.; the Evangelical Churches in Baden, V.46 and Hesse-Nassau, IV.134; Church of Scotland, I.95; Union of Welsh Independents, III.272f.; United Church of Christ in Japan, II.289; Church of England, III.44, the Anglican Churches in Canada, II.39 and New Zealand, II.66; and, from another direction, the Roman Catholic Church, VI.18-21.

4. A final general remark concerns the generosity and gratitude with which many churches coming from the Reformation and Free churches particularly, express their readiness to have their understanding, and above all their practice, of the Lord's supper challenged and enriched by the more "catholic" insights of the Lima text drawn from the wider Tradition, provided the "evangelical" doctrine is maintained. "The text offers several areas for theological growth among Disciples of Christ as we seek to build upon our historic teachings related to the Lord's supper, and as we seek with other churches to reclaim the eucharist as central to the church's life and witness" (Christian Church (Disciples of Christ), USA and Canada, I.117). It is "illuminating for our faith" (American Baptist Churches in the USA, III.260). Lima "unfolds aspects of the Lord's supper which are hardly effective or are missing in our understanding and practice" (Church of Lippe, VI.71). "We welcome what other churches have to tell us from their tradition and practice in celebrating the Lord's supper as this emerges from BEM. It can correct bias and faulty elements in our historical development and can remind us of the meaning of the Lord's supper as that was rediscovered in the Reformation. Here we are thinking of such themes as the joyful celebration of Easter, *epiklesis* (invocation of the Holy Spirit), fellowship, reconciliation, sharing, and ethical concepts and eschatological and cosmic dimensions in the celebration of the Lord's supper" (Swiss Protestant Church Federation, VI.81).[11]

2. The institution of the eucharist (E.1)

5. The opening declaration of Christ's institution of the eucharist at the Last Supper is welcomed both for its historical rootage of the sacrament and for its emphasis on the eucharist's character as a "gift from the Lord".[12] The Apostolic Catholic Assyrian Church of the East cites the narrative of the institution in a composite form, twice including the Matthaean phrase "remission of sins" (III.29). This emphasis matches a

---

[11] See further expressions of such appreciation, e.g., from the Baptist Union of Denmark, III.249; the Church of the Brethren, USA, VI.108f.; Church of North India, II.72; United Reformed Church in the United Kingdom, I.105; the Evangelical Churches of Kurhessen-Waldeck, V.96f., and the GDR, V.132; the Lutheran Churches of Iceland, IV.64, North Elbia, I.43, Norway, II.113, and Sweden, II.130f. On stimulus to more frequent celebration of the Lord's supper, see below, paragraph 39.

[12] Cf. for example Roman Catholic Church, VI.17; Church of England, III.42; Evangelical Lutheran Church of Hanover, IV.50; Methodist Churches in the GDR, IV.170, and the FRG, IV.176.

complaint on the part of Reformation churches that this benefit of communion, the forgiveness of sins, comes off short in the text as a whole.[13] Cf. "Clarifications", B.7.

6. The wider location of the eucharist in relation also to the other significant meals of Jesus during his earthly ministry and after his resurrection shows that the Lima text "take[s] into account the findings of modern exegetics in a balanced way" (Evangelical Lutheran Church in Bavaria, IV.31).[14] Generally approved, too, are the eucharist's "salvation-historical connection with the Old Testament and also its eschatological implications" (Presbyterian Church of Korea, II.161).[15]

7. The mention of "liturgy", "sacrament", "sign" and "symbol" towards the end of E.1 provokes the first of many rounds of comments on the nature and efficacy of the Lord's supper.[16] These matters are addressed in "Clarifications", B.1-3.

8. The many names used by churches for the eucharist elicit several comments that it would have been appropriate and wise for BEM to

---

[13] It is a heavy preponderance of Lutheran churches which call for more weight on the forgiveness of sins: North Elbia, I.46f., American Lutheran Church, II.81,82, Hungary, III.129, Missouri Synod, III.137, Austria, IV.18, Bavaria, IV.32, Hanover, IV.52, Romania, IV.87f., Württemberg, V.27, Independent Evangelical Lutheran Church, FRG, VI.55. They are joined by the Evangelical Churches of Westphalia, IV.144, Baden, V.47, the Rhineland, V.78, Kurhessen-Waldeck, V.99, River Plate, Argentina, V.176, and Lippe, VI.72; by the European Continental Province of the Moravian Church, VI.119; and by the Church of England, III.48. Somewhat contrariwise, the Roman Catholic response notes that "the 'assurance of the forgiveness of sins' [E.2] through the eucharist is preconditioned by the state of reconciliation with God in the church. This points to the need of previous reconciliation of sinners (cf. 1 Cor. 11:28). In our understanding the previous reconciliation would take place through the sacrament of penance" (VI.18).

[14] The reference to Jesus' other meals is also welcomed, e.g., by the (Lutheran) Church of Denmark, III.110; the Reformed Churches in the Netherlands, IV.105; Churches of Christ in Australia, II.269. However, the (Anglican) Church of Ireland considers these to have "minimal significance in our understanding of the sacrament" (I.66), and the Lutheran Church of Australia believes that "this fails to give the supper its specific anchorage in the death, the cross of Christ" (II.90).

[15] See also e.g. United Church of Christ in Japan, (II.289: "a rich sacramental incorporating of the entire salvation history"); Federation of Evangelical Churches in the GDR, V.132, and the Baptists in the GDR, IV.195.

[16] So, from very varied points of view, the Baptist Union of Great Britain, I.71; Church of Scotland, I:97; Christian Church, Disciples of Christ, USA, I.114; Lutheran Church of Australia, II.90f.; Seventh Day Adventists, II.341f.; the Romanian Orthodox Church, III.7; Methodist Church in the GDR, IV.168; the British Quakers, IV.220-22; Salvation Army, IV.242-46.

employ a greater variety in its own usage. Protestant churches, in particular, miss an emphasis on "the Lord's supper".[17] On this matter cf. "Clarifications", B.1.

9. The designation of the eucharist as "the central act of the Church's worship" appears to many Reformation as well as some Free churches to threaten the integrity of the service of the word (scripture reading, preaching, prayers).[18] Some, however, noting that the eucharist "always includes both word and sacrament" (E.3; cf. E.12,27), find that such correspondence to the incarnate word makes the Lord's supper an appropriate norm of Christian worship: "God's effectual word is there revealed, proclaimed, heard, seen and tasted" (United Methodist Church, USA, II.188). The Reformed Churches in the Netherlands state: "The indissoluble bond between word and sacrament, preaching and celebration in the eucharist, which Lima assumes, should be seen as a lesson for *all* traditions" (IV.108).[19] See further "Clarifications", B.2. The question of the eucharist's "centrality" is connected to that of the frequency of its celebration, which is treated below with reference to E.30-31 (para. 39).

3. The meaning of the eucharist (E.2-26)

10. Approval is frequently expressed, or tacitly given, for the exposition of the eucharist's meaning according to the fivefold structure that marks the ancient creeds and some classical anaphoras: Father (E.3-4), Son (E.5-13), Holy Spirit (E.14-18), church (E.19-21), kingdom (E.22-

---

[17] Some examples are Church of Scotland, I.95; Presbyterian Church in Ireland, III.211; Swiss Protestant Church Federation, VI.83; Waldensian Church of the River Plate, Uruguay, IV.121; United Protestant Church of Belgium, III.172; Moravian Church of Continental Europe, VI.119; Evangelical Church of the Augsburg Confession in Austria, IV.18.

[18] So e.g. the Baptist Union of Great Britain, I.76; United German Mennonite Congregations, VI.127; American Lutheran Church, II.82, and Lutheran Churches in Austria, IV.18, France, III.161, and Württemberg, V.26f.; the Evangelical Churches in the GDR, V.133, and the River Plate, Argentina, V.176f.; Reformed Church in America, II.146; Evangelical Church of the Helvetic Confession in Austria (mimeographed document); United Protestant Church of Belgium, III.172; United Church of Christ in Japan, II.289; United Methodist Church in the FRG, IV.178, and in Central and Southern Europe, II.205.

[19] Approval for the centrality of the eucharist comes, e.g., from the Bulgarian Orthodox Church, II.17; Lutheran Church of North Elbia, I.44; Reformed Church of Hungary, V.162; Scottish Episcopal Church, II.54; Episcopal Church in the USA, II.59f.; United Church of Canada, II.280.

26). The Church of England notes: "A principal source of strength in the text is the central and longest section which sets forth the meaning of the eucharist in relation to the doctrines of the Trinity (as thanksgiving to the Father, as memorial of Christ, and as invocation of the Spirit), of the Church and of eschatology. This particular structure provides a welcome balance and harmony to eucharistic theology" (III.42).[20] The Christological origin and focus of this fivefold pattern is recognized to be assured in the introductory paragraph E.2 and elsewhere.[21]

a) The eucharist as thanksgiving to the Father (E.3-4)

11. Many churches welcome a restoration of the full cosmic range of the intended "sacrifice of praise", whose expression had become rather curtailed in some liturgies.[22] The Christological focus already recognized requires that the mediation of Christ be maintained, as is done for the movement towards God in E.4.[23]

12. While some Reformation churches are suspicious lest the opening emphasis on thanksgiving make of the Lord's supper too much of a "work

---

[20] The United Methodist Church, USA (II.188): "BEM carefully shows how the eucharist, considered in its wholeness, expresses the historic faith in the unity of God's activity by the three persons." Cf. also Roman Catholic Church (VI.16): "The presentation of the mystery of the eucharist follows the flow of classical eucharistic liturgies..." Note also, e.g., Bulgarian Orthodox Church, II.17; Finnish Orthodox Church, II.27; Romanian Orthodox Church, III.6f.; Orthodox Church in America, III.18f.; Mar Thoma Church, IV.8-10; (Anglican) Church of Ceylon, IV.15; Lutheran Churches of France, III.159, and Iceland, IV.62; Federation of Evangelical Churches in the GDR, V.132; Presbyterian Churches in Ghana, VI.96, Korea, II.161f., and North-West Germany, IV.95; Evangelical Church of the Czech Brethren, IV.112; Methodist Church in Southern Africa, II.238; American Baptist Churches in the USA, III.260; Christian Church, Disciples of Christ, USA and Canada, I.116; Church of Jesus Christ in Madagascar, III.187.

[21] So the Roman Catholic Church, VI.16; the Lutheran Churches of Bavaria, IV.31f., Hanover, IV.50f., Iceland, IV.62, Norway, II.112, and Württemberg, V.25f.; the Evangelical Churches of Baden, V.42, and the Rhineland, V.76. The Uniting Church in Australia has some reservations in this respect (IV.158: "... a clear expression of the faith of the church through the ages would emphasize that the thanksgiving to the Father at the eucharistic celebration falls on the death and resurrection of Jesus Christ").

[22] See, for example, the comment of the Church of South India, II.76, as well as the related responses listed in note 6.

[23] Nevertheless, the United Methodist Church in Central and Southern Europe considers that "the Christological component of the thanksgiving in which the gathered congregation thanks the Father for sending the Son into the world, and for acting through the Son for the salvation of the world, although present, is short-changed" (II.205).

of the church",[24] most (including some of the critical ones, recognize that gratitude is an appropriate response "to the Father for everything accomplished in creation, redemption and sanctification, for everything accomplished by God now in the church and in the world in spite of the sins of human beings, for everything that God will accomplish in bringing the kingdom to fulfilment" (E.3).

b) The eucharist as anamnesis *or memorial of Christ (E.5-13)*

13. The connection between section B, "The Memorial of Christ" *(anamnesis)*, and section C, "Invocation of the Spirit" *(epiklesis)*, is particularly close. The Russian Orthodox Church says: "We note again with satisfaction the importance of the document's pointing to the need for not only *anamnesis* but also *epiklesis* which are essentially inseparable" (II.7). This is expressed by the United Methodist Church in the USA in this way: "In terms of the congregation's appropriation of the reality of Christ's presence, the *anamnesis* (memorial, remembrance, representation) means that past, present and future coincide in the sacramental event. All that Jesus Christ means in his person and redemptive work is brought forth from history to our present experience which is also a foretaste of the future fulfilment of God's unobstructed reign. And this presence is made to be a reality for us by the working of God's Spirit, whom we 'call down' *(epiklesis)* by invocation, both upon the gifts and upon the people" (II.188).[25] It is a characteristic Orthodox concern that Christ never be without the accompaniment of the Holy Spirit.[26] It is a

---

[24] This comment is preponderantly Lutheran in origin: American Lutheran Church, II.82; Missouri Synod, III.135; Lutheran Churches in Austria, IV.10, Denmark, III.111, Estonia, IV.13, Hanover, IV.51f., Hungary, III.129, Württemberg, V.27; Independent Evangelical Lutheran, FRG, VI.55. They are joined by the Evangelical Churches in Baden, V.46f., Berlin-Brandenburg, VI.63, the GDR, V.133, Rhineland, V.76,78, and Westphalia, IV.143; Presbyterian Church in Rwanda, III.183; United Church of Christ, USA, II.329; and the Methodist Churches in the GDR, IV.170, and the FRG, IV.178. These criticisms are sometimes aimed also at the mention of the church's "intercession" in E.8.

[25] Cf. Bulgarian Orthodox Church, II.18; Finnish Orthodox Church, II.27; Romanian Orthodox Church, III.7; Orthodox Church in America, II.18; Malankara Orthodox Syrian Church, V.5; Roman Catholic Church, VI.21,22; Lutheran Churches of North Elbia, I.43f., Norway, II.114, Finland, III.120f., France, III.150f.; the Evangelical Churches in the GDR, V.135; Church of England, III.44f.; Baptist Union of Sweden, IV.207.

[26] Bulgarian Orthodox Church (II.18: "The *anamnesis* should be related directly to the action of the Holy Spirit because it is precisely through the Spirit that all Christ has accomplished once and for ever is being actualized in the holy eucharist"); Finnish Orthodox Church (II.27: the document "in many respects correctly understands the role of *epiklesis* for the

characteristic Lutheran concern that the Holy Spirit never appear independently of the Word and his words.[27] On these concerns see further paragraphs 24,28-30, and "Clarifications", B.4.

14. While some doubts remain lest the notion of *anamnesis* should have been overextended,[28] there is a widespread recognition that this scriptural and liturgical category of "dynamic memorial", as recovered in twentieth-century biblical and patristic scholarship (see "Clarifications", B.4) provides a promising way of overcoming some old controversies.[29] If the eucharist can be recognized as "the memorial of the crucified and risen Christ, i.e., the living and effective sign of his sacrifice, accomplished once and for all on the cross and still operative on behalf of all humankind" (E.5), then hope has appeared for greater agreement on matters to do with the presence and sacrifice of Christ. Nevertheless, some ambiguities and inadequacies are detected in the Lima text, although the churches' respective proposals for their resolution would sometimes appear to pull in opposed directions.

c) Presence of Christ

15. The broad general agreement and the many requests for further precision have been noticed already in paragraph 3 and notes 7 and 8.

16. The original commentary to E.13 called on the churches to decide whether differences in the understanding of Christ's eucharistic presence

---

eucharist. The *anamnesis* cannot be separated from the *epiklesis*"); Romanian Orthodox Church (III.7: "The real presence of Christ in the eucharist is acknowledged, but the statement 'the *anamnesis* of Christ is the very content of the eucharistic meal' (E.12) shifts importance from the real presence of Christ onto *anamnesis* or a memorial presence of Christ, without emphasizing the fundamental unity of *anamnesis* and *epiklesis*, that is, the link between the work of the Son and that of the Holy Spirit in the eucharist").

[27] Lutheran Churches of Norway, II.114f., Sweden, II.131f., Finland, III.122, Missouri Synod, III.136; cf. Evangelical Church of the Rhineland, V.78f.

[28] The Anglican Churches of the Southern Cone, I.59 and Australia, II.34; the American Lutheran Church, II.82 and the Missouri Synod, III.136; Evangelical Church of the Rhineland, V.79; Czech Brethren, IV.113; Scottish Baptist Union, III.238; Union of Welsh Independents, III.272.

[29] Some examples are: Roman Catholic Church, VI.19; Bulgarian Orthodox Church, II.18; Church of England, III.43f.; Methodist Churches in Great Britain, II.215, and Southern Africa, II.239; Lutheran Churches in the Netherlands, V.20, and Romania, IV.85,87; Evangelical Churches in the GDR, V.134; Presbyterian Church of Wales, II.170; Moravian Church in America, Southern Province, II.257; American Baptist Churches in the USA, III.260; Christian Church, Disciples of Christ, USA and Canada, I.117; Churches of Christ in Australia, II.270.

could be "accommodated within the convergence formulated in the text". The Church of North India "appreciates... this statement for its careful avoidance of such controversial terms as 'transubstantiation', 'transignification', etc., and focuses attention on the central significance and experiential aspect of the eucharist in terms of the 'real presence' of Christ in this sacrament, which is likely to be acceptable to most of the WCC member churches as a common understanding of the eucharist" (II.72).

17. On one side, however, the Presbyterian Church of Wales considers that the text "does not give sufficient weight to the position that excludes certain modes of presence in the eucharist... We would firmly resist any suggestion of a change in the essential nature of the elements of bread and wine" (II.169,171). The Union of Evangelical Free Churches in the GDR (Baptist) comments: "We affirm the real presence of Christ, but we conceive of it in a pneumatic way... The *is* of the words of institution does not want to be understood as a 'transubstantiation' (in the hour of institution Jesus is still seated bodily in the midst of his disciples and his blood has not yet been shed; consequently, he cannot mean to say that the bread is his body and the cup is his blood). The *is* is only a device of translation and has no place in Jesus' own saying. In the words of the institution of the eucharist, the copula-forms have quite obviously a figurative sense. Therefore, it is not the substance of bread and wine, but rather the act of the breaking of the bread and the offering of wine which is the saving sign standing in correlation to the saving surrender of the body and blood of Christ" (IV.196f.; cf. Baptist Union of Scotland, III.236f.).

18. From another side, the Roman Catholic Church notes that "for the Catholic doctrine, the *conversion* of the elements is a matter of faith and is only open to possible new theological explanations as to the 'how' of the intrinsic change. The content of the word 'transubstantiation' ought to be expressed without ambiguity. For Catholics this is a central mystery of faith, and they cannot accept expressions that are ambiguous. Thus it would seem that the differences as explained here cannot be accommodated within the convergence formulated in the text itself. Further work must be done on this" (VI.22). The North Elbian Evangelical Lutheran Church "affirm[s] emphatically that the miracle of the eucharist, the *presence of Christ's body and blood* is celebrated 'in, with and under' bread and wine" (I.45). The Lutheran Church Missouri Synod says that "the intent of Lutheranism's traditional 'in, with and under'" was "to avoid philosophical speculation about the precise nature of the mystery" (III.137).

19. Several Orthodox responses take exception to the phrase "sacramental signs" in this connection. Thus the Russian Orthodox Church

writes: "The bread and wine are declared to be only 'the sacramental signs of Christ's body and blood' (E.15); whereas the Orthodox Church, basing itself on the Saviour's institutional statement (Matt. 26:26-28), believes that the bread is really and truly and essentially itself the body of the Lord and the wine is itself the blood of the Lord. According to St John of Damascus, 'the body is truly united with the Godhead; themselves the bread and wine are transubstantiated into the body and blood of God'" (*De Fide Orthodoxa* IV.C 13 (II.8)).[30]

20. Most would agree with BEM that it is the one Christ himself who is present as he "fulfills in a variety of ways his promise to be always with his own even to the end of the world" (E.13), yet much comment was provoked by the statement that "Christ's mode of presence in the eucharist is unique" (E.13). The Baptist Union of Great Britain and Ireland finds the word "unique" to be "question-begging" (I.76), and several other Protestant responses ask for a clarification of its meaning.[31] The chief objection is to any suggestion that Christ's presence in the eucharist may be *qualitatively superior* to his presence in another mode.[32] This appears to be the line of thinking represented by the comments of the Old Catholic Church of Switzerland on the relation between word and sacrament: "On the one hand it should be mentioned that the eucharist is to be understood as coming from the word and on the other hand that in the eucharist it is experienced *most intensively* that the word became flesh in Christ, thus has entered into the whole reality of human life and that it effects visible corporeal communion" (V.10; emphasis added). With regard to several concerns raised about the understanding of "presence" see "Clarifications", B.5.

d) Sacrifice of Christ

21. That the churches raised questions concerning the sacrificial character of the eucharistic action was shown already in paragraphs 3 and 12.

---

[30] Cf. Bulgarian Orthodox Church, II.17f.; Finnish Orthodox Church, II.27; Romanian Orthodox Church, III.7f.

[31] Church of South India, II.77; Methodist Church of Great Britain, II.223; Waldensian and Methodist Churches in Italy, II.249f. It causes the United Church of Canada to fear that "the convergence on the doctrine of 'real presence', which the text affirms, may be more apparent than real" (II.281).

[32] So the Lutherans in France, III.153 and Oldenburg, IV.77; the Methodists in Great Britain, II.223, the GDR, IV.170, and the FRG, IV.178; Union of Welsh Independents, III.273.

22. Almost all responses from the Reformation and Free churches appear to agree with the Reformed Churches of the Netherlands that "the uniqueness and unrepeatable nature of Christ's saving work" is sufficiently respected in BEM (IV.105).[33] The Mar Thoma Church adds to this that "the eschatological reality" of the unrepeatable act of God in Christ "needs to be 'realized' in historical contemporaneity repeatedly" (IV.9).

23. On one side, however, the Waldensian Church of the River Plate objects to the original commentary to E.8 for saying "that 'there is only one expiation, that of the unique sacrifice of the cross, made actual in the eucharist and presented before the Father in the intercession of Christ and of the church for all humanity', because the sacrifice of Jesus Christ cannot be actualized, made actual, but only recalled *(anamnesis)*, and it cannot be said that the church can 'present', 'offer' anything to the Father, but that it is God himself who offers in Jesus Christ and it is the church that receives and is sent to bear witness to Jesus Christ among other people" (IV.120).

24. On the other hand, the Romanian Orthodox Church considers that "the document separates the eucharist from the economy of salvation" by declaring that the incarnation, life, death, resurrection and ascension of Christ "are unique and can neither be repeated nor prolonged" (E.8); rather the eucharist is to be understood "as a permanent updating of the entire economy of salvation in the church, through Christ, in the Holy Spirit" (III.8). The Bulgarian Orthodox Church finds in E.8 "very appropriately pointed out the unity and uniqueness of the sacrifice of Christ and of all that the Son of God has done with his incarnation, life, passion, death, resurrection and ascension. This is a safeguard against the misbelief of conceiving the holy eucharist as being a repetition or a prolongation of that sacrifice and of the events indicated in E.8." But nor is the eucharist "a mental memorial of something that had been accomplished in the past", for "through the Spirit... all that Christ has accomplished once and forever is being actualized in the eucharist" (III.18).

25. The Roman Catholic response declares that "the connection established [by BEM] between the sacrifice of the cross and the eucharist corresponds to Catholic understanding" (VI.19). However, the Roman

---

[33] For example: the Lutheran Churches in Finland, III.120, France, III.160, and Württemberg, V.26; the Evangelical Churches in Baden, V.42, and Lippe, VI.7; Church of Scotland, I.89, Reformed Church in America, II.147; Church in Wales, III.83f.; the United Methodist Church, USA, II.189, the Methodists in Ireland, II.233, and the GDR, IV.70; Uniting Church in Australia, IV.157f.

Catholic response finds difficulty in some aspects of the use BEM makes of "intercession" in connection with the sacrificial character of the eucharist: "The link between the historical event of the cross and the present efficacy of that event is the crucified and risen Lord, established as High Priest and 'Intercessor'. In this perspective it is correct to say that the 'events' of Christ's life, as historical events, were caught up in the flow of time and cannot be repeated 'or prolonged'. But since the High Priest is the crucified and risen Lord, his offering of self on the cross can be said to be 'made eternal'. His glorified body is the body of the Lord offered once-for-all. Consequently, it does not seem to do justice to the reality of Christ's sacrifice to describe the continuity of Christ's saving work only in terms of simple 'intercession'. Correspondingly, the description of the church's activity in the eucharist as thanksgiving and intercession needs to be filled out by some reference to the self-offering of the participants of the eucharist, made in union with the eternal 'self-offering' of Christ. E.9-11 can be read in such a way that this notion is included. The suggestion is made (E.8 comm.) that Catholic doctrine's references to the eucharist as propitiatory sacrifice be understood in terms of intercession. But Catholics would ask: Is it sufficient to describe the role of Christ, in the 'application of the propitiatory effects of the cross', as 'intercessor'?" (VI.20).

26. Again, further exploration of the category of *anamnesis* employed by BEM may help to show that due recognition of the uniqueness of Christ's work and an acknowledgment of the sacrificial character of the eucharist may not be so contradictory as historical controversies have made them out to be. For further clarification see "Clarifications", B.6.

e) The eucharist as invocation of the Spirit (E.14-18)

27. As noted above in paragraph 13, many responses recognize that the "invocation of the Spirit" *(epiklesis)* must be in closest correlation to the "memorial of Christ" *(anamnesis)*. See also "Clarifications", B.4.

28. Orthodox and some Reformed responses welcome BEM's recognition of the role of the Holy Spirit in the Lord's supper as generally in line with their own tradition, even if needing some further clarification.[34]

---

[34] Russian Orthodox Church, II.7; Finnish Orthodox Church, II.27; Romanian Orthodox Church, III.7f.; Malankara Orthodox Syrian Church, V.5; Mar Thoma Church, IV.9f. Among the Reformed: Presbyterian Church of Cameroon, I.82; Presbyterian Church of Ireland, III.210; Reformed Churches of the Netherlands, IV.105; Swiss Protestant Church Federation, VI.83.

Approval comes, however, from other quarters also, where the pneumatological dimension of the eucharist has not always been strongly underlined.[35] Thus the Anglican Church of Canada notes that "the emphasis on *epiklesis* not only restores the importance of the role of the Holy Spirit in the operation of the sacraments, but also makes it clear that the sacraments are prayer actions and not mechanical means of grace" (II.39). And the Evangelical Lutheran Church in Bavaria: "In [the efficacy of the Holy Ghost] we see expressed that the church does not control the gift of the sacrament, but entreats the presence of God. This wards off at the same time a magical understanding of the speaking of the *verba testamenti*" (IV.32; cf. Federation of Evangelical Churches in the GDR, V.135).

29. However, a number of responses, from the Anglican and especially the Lutheran tradition, doubt or reject a form of *epiklesis* that was "constitutive" or invoked the Holy Spirit upon the elements.[36]

30. Thus several Lutheran responses assert the sufficiency of the Word and his words in making Christ present.[37] The sharpest expression comes from the Evangelical Lutheran Church in the Netherlands: "Our main objection is to E.14. In it the Holy Spirit's office is elevated to that of a mediating agent; as being someone necessary for the *realis presentia Christi* and the fulfilment of the 'promise in the words of institution'... In our view, however, the sacrament is governed neither by the ministry nor by the Spirit, but solely by the word. It is none other than *verbum visible*. The word is an active word" (V.21). The same church, however, accepts E.17, which it finds to match a prayer in the Lutheran liturgy of Sweden: "Send thy Spirit into our hearts that he may kindle in us a lively faith and prepare us rightly to celebrate the memorial of our Saviour and receive him when he comes to us in his holy supper" (V.21). See further "Clarifications", B.4.

---

[35] Cf. e.g. Roman Catholic Church, VI.21-22; Church of England, III.45; Lutheran Churches of Finland, III.121f. (with reservations), France, III.158f., and Sweden, II.131f. (hesitantly); Evangelical Churches of the Rhineland, V.78, and the River Plate, Argentina, V.176; United Methodist Church, USA, II.188, 191); Methodist Church of Southern Africa, II.239; United Church of Canada, II.280; Baptist Union of Sweden, IV.207.

[36] Cf. e.g. Anglican Churches of Australia, II.34 and Canada, II.43f.; American Lutheran Church, II.82; Lutheran Churches in Austria, IV.18, and Estonia, IV.43f.; also Evangelical Churches in Kurhessen-Waldeck, V.99, and Westphalia, IV.145; Union of Welsh Independents, III.274. On the other hand, the Anglican Church in New Zealand (II.66) and the Evangelical Church in Hesse and Nassau (IV.134) approve of an invocation of the Holy Spirit upon both the community and the elements.

[37] Lutheran Churches of Finland, III.122, Norway, II.115, Sweden, II.131; Austria, IV.18, Estonia, IV.43, Hanover, IV.52.

f) The eucharist as communion of the faithful (E.19-21)

31. The link established by E.19 between "each local eucharistic celebration" and "the whole church" is acknowledged in many responses, but — with the notable exception of the Old Catholic Church of Switzerland (V.15f.) — not much pursued.[38] The Roman Catholic Church points out that questions of ministry and authority are thereby raised, which can only be treated in a wider ecclesiological discussion of "catholicity" (VI.19f., 23).

32. E.20 provoked some of the sharpest and most colourful reactions. Some felt that this was where the document was most "earthed" and would have liked to see this more "passionate" approach governing the whole text.[39] Others considered the text imprecise: is "reconciliation and sharing among all those regarded as brothers and sisters in the one family of God" a *condition* or a *consequence* of the eucharist celebration and communion?[40] Which "confessional oppositions" are "unjustifiable"?[41] Some Lutheran responses fear in E.20, as elsewhere, an unacceptable mixture of law and gospel.[42] See further "Clarifications", B.8 and 9.

g) The eucharist as meal of the kingdom (E.22-26)

33. BEM's acknowledgment of the eschatological dimension of the Lord's supper finds very widespread approval, whether the accent be

---

[38] For example: Bulgarian Orthodox Church, II.18f.; Church of England, III.48; Lutheran Churches of Finland, III.120, and North Elbia, I.44; Baptists in Denmark, III.250, and the GDR, IV.196; Seventh Day Adventists, II.342.

[39] The paragraph finds general approval from, for example, the Lutheran Church in America, I.37; Church of South India, II.77; Presbyterian Church of Korea, II.162; United Methodist Church, USA, II.192; United Church of Christ, USA, II.329; Church of England, III.47f.; Presbyterian Church, USA, III.197f.; Mar Thoma Church, IV.10; Waldensian Church of the River Plate, Uruguay, IV.120f.; Burma Baptist Convention, IV.188; Federation of Evangelical Churches in the GDR, V.136; Reformed Church in Hungary, V.162.

[40] Lutheran Church of Hanover, IV.52; Moravian Church in Great Britain and Ireland, III.286; Union of Welsh Independents, III.275f.

[41] Orthodox Church in America, III.19f.; Lutheran Church Missouri Synod, III.138; Union of Welsh Independents, III.276.

[42] Most sharply, the Lutheran Church of Australia: "a mixture of law and gospel which we cannot accept" (II.91). Cf. also the Lutheran Church Missouri Synod, III.137f., and the Independent Evangelical Lutheran Church in the FRG, VI.55. More gently, the concern about the relation between law and gospel comes to expression in other Lutheran responses concerning the gift of God and the actions of the church.

placed on joy and hope, or on mission and service, or on the anticipation of the parousia and the feast of the kingdom.[43]

34. The Episcopal Church, USA discerns that "both of two eschatologies seem to be operating through the whole of BEM: one holds that the kingdom is to come, whereas the other maintains that in Jesus the kingdom of God has arrived, and we are now growing towards its fullness" (II.62; cf. Evangelical Church of the Rhineland, V.82). For its part, the Evangelical Lutheran Church of North Elbia welcomes in E.22-26 "the thankful reverent experience of the present operation of the eschatological future of God's kingdom" (I.44). The Anglican Church of Australia calls for further exploration of the "role... sacraments... play in the consummation of the kingdom" (II.32).

35. Few responses comment on the "communion with all the saints and martyrs" which had been maintained in E.11. While one or two reject it, several Reformation churches welcome this theme.[44] The Lutheran Church of Estonia states: "Death does not break up the community of believers... For us the eucharist must be the sensible expression of unity, which is not separated by death" (IV.46).

4. The celebration of the eucharist (E.27-33)

36. The enumeration in E.27 of the various elements historically found in eucharistic liturgies — admittedly "in varying sequence and of diverse importance" — is welcomed by some Protestant churches as a source for enriching their own practice.[45] Others fear an "overloading" beyond what is necessary and sufficient.[46]

---

[43] Notably the Roman Catholic Church, VI.17,19,23f.; Orthodox Church in America, III.18; Mar Thoma Church, IV.10; Church of England, III.47; Lutheran Churches of Estonia, IV.46, Finland, III.21, Württemberg, V.26, and the Independent Evangelical Lutheran Church in the FRG, VI.56; Presbyterian Church of Korea, II.62; the Reformed Churches of the Netherlands, IV.105; Methodist Churches in Ireland, II.233, and Southern Africa, II.239; Moravian Church, Continental Europe, VI.118.

[44] So, for instance, the Czech Brethren, IV.114; Waldensian Church of the River Plate, Uruguay, IV.120; Church of the Augsburg Confession, Romania, IV.87.

[45] For example, Evangelical Lutheran Church of North Elbia, I.47; Evangelical Church in Berlin-Brandenburg, VI.62; United Methodist Church, USA, II.189. Doubtless the "enrichment" recognized in paragraph 4 and note 11 above also has implications for the liturgical celebration.

[46] Christian Church, Disciples of Christ, USA and Canada, I.117; Presbyterian Church of Ireland, III.213; Waldensian Church of the River Plate, Uruguay, IV.121; Evangelical Church of the Rhineland, V.83; Swiss Protestant Church Federation, VI.82.

37. Few responses comment on the question of the use of local food and drink other than bread and wine (E.28, comm.). The Methodist Church of Nigeria emphasizes: "We have found reason to stress that elements and instruments in the eucharist ought to take into consideration the local situation" (mimeographed document). The Melanesian Council of Churches simply reports that "the elements of bread and wine... are unfamiliar and cause both material and symbolic difficulties, whereas coconut milk or *kaukau* (sweet potato) are traditionally significant and may be more readily available. Some churches approve of the use of such substances as elements" (V.182); and the (Anglican) Church of the Province of New Zealand remarks that the issue "may well be raised within our own Province which includes the diocese in Polynesia" (II.67). Other Anglican churches express great caution (Canada, 11.39, USA, II.60, Wales, III.91, Ireland, I.67), as does the Church of South India: "The symbol should be obvious and meaningful. We have no problem with any type of bread, but it may be difficult to take the coconut water and say, 'This is the blood of Christ'" (II.77)[47] The Apostolic Catholic Assyrian Church of the East observes that "the matter of this sacrament Christ ordained to be of wheat and wine as being most fit to represent body and blood" (III.29). And the Lutheran Church in Romania is "prompted to insist that at the Lord's supper only grape wine — and as far as possible good pure wine — should be used" (IV.87).

38. The recognition in E.29 of Christ as the host at his own supper is widely welcomed,[48] often set in conjunction with E.2 and other places where Christ is also the food, both giver and gift.[49] The observation of E.29 that "in most churches, [Christ's] presidency is signified by an ordained minister" is felt to remain at an unsatisfactory phenomenological level. Reasons should have been given for the reservation, or not, of this role to the bishop, presbyter or pastor.[50]

---

[47] Cautious also is the Moravian Church in America, Southern Province, II.257.

[48] Cf. e.g. Russian Orthodox Church, II.7; Reformed Church of Alsace and Lorraine, III.166; Presbyterian Church of Ireland, III.20; Baptist Union of Scotland, III.237.

[49] Roman Catholic Church, VI.17f.,19; Lutheran Churches of Hanover, IV.50, Iceland, IV.62, Württemberg, V.25f.; Evangelical Churches of Baden, V.41, and the GDR, V.132.

[50] So, from various angles (sometimes opposed), e.g. the Church of Ireland, I.67; Christian Church, Disciples of Christ, USA, I.119; Russian Orthodox Church, II.8; Episcopal Church, USA, II.60; (Anglican) Church of the Province of South Africa, III.103; the Lutheran Churches of France, III.152; Reformed Church of Alsace and Lorraine, III.166; Christian Church, Disciples of Christ, Canada, III.265; Uniting Church in Australia, IV.160; Swiss Old Catholic Church, V.12,14; Federation of Evangelical Churches in the GDR, V.137; Roman Catholic Church, VI.24.

39. While continuing to affirm the integrity of a preaching service, many Reformation and Free churches see themselves challenged by E.30-31 to a more frequent, even weekly, celebration of the Lord's supper.[51] The Swiss Protestant Church Federation recognizes that "celebration every Sunday is in line with the biblical tradition" (VI.83). Noting that "formerly many congregations... celebrated the Lord's supper only on the first Sunday of each month", the Church of Jesus Christ in Madagascar reports that "at present, thanks to BEM, the CJCM accepts the principle of celebrating the eucharist every Sunday. For the preaching of the word should not be separated from the sacraments" (III.187f.). Several Orthodox churches recognize the need for more frequent communion, provided due spiritual and moral preparation has taken place.[52] The Orthodox Church in America reports in its own life "a significant renewal in recent years in regard to the eucharist", thanks in part to "the work of many theologians, some of whom have influenced the WCC Faith and Order Commission's statement on BEM" (III.18).

40. The Roman Catholic Church finds difficulty with the typology of positions regarding presence and reservation in E.32: "A distinction is made (E.32) between churches, which stress 'that Christ's presence in the consecrated elements continues after the celebration', and others, which place 'the main emphasis on the act of celebration itself and on the consumption of the elements in the act of communion'. The Catholic Church agrees with the first position and also agrees with what is said positively about the second position. She only disagrees with those who deny the duration of the real presence after the celebration. And we would ask, if one denies the duration of the real presence after the celebration, what does this signify for one's understanding of real presence and the reality of the conversion? Therefore, it would have been useful to indicate the deeper ecclesiological, sacramental and eschatological grounds for the ancient practice of reservation of the consecrated species. While that text

---

[51] Cf. e.g. Episcopal Church, USA, II.59; Scottish Episcopal Church, II.54; Lutheran Church in America, I.36; Lutheran Church Missouri-Synod, II.135; Lutheran Churches of Canada, II.104, Hungary, III.129, and Oldenburg, IV.78; Evangelical Churches of Baden, V.47, Berlin-Brandenburg, VI.61, the GDR, V.134; Church of Scotland, I.94; Reformed Church of Alsace and Lorraine, III.166; United Methodist Church, USA, II.189; Methodist Churches in Ireland, II.233, and the FRG, IV.178; Baptist Union of Scotland, III.239. The Presbyterian Church of Canada warns against overfamiliarity (II.156).

[52] Russian Orthodox Church, II.7,11; Bulgarian Orthodox Church, II.14,19; Finnish Orthodox Church, II.27).

states that 'the best way of showing respect for the elements... is by their consumption, without excluding their use for communion of the sick', we would add to this that the various forms of eucharistic worship, properly done, are also legitimate and praiseworthy ways of acknowledging the continuing presence of Christ in the eucharist" (VI.24f.). Some Reformation churches are reluctant to countenance any practice that would make adoration of the species even a possibility.[53]

41. The Bulgarian Church sees E.33 as "indirectly" raising the question of "intercommunion" and responds that "eucharistic communion" is "the climax and crown", possible "only on the basis of a unity in the confession of the faith" (II.19f.). The Russian (II.5), Finnish (II.27), and Romanian (III.8) Orthodox churches agree that that moment has not yet been reached, as does the Roman Catholic Church (VI.25,38). The (Lutheran) Church of Norway does not "feel that what is stated in the BEM document yet provides an adequate basis for full eucharistic community between the churches involved"; yet this church has "long practised the principle of open communion which means that members from other churches are admitted to our church's celebration of the eucharist" (II.116). The Scottish Episcopal Church recognizes in the eucharist section of BEM a consensus which is "sufficient agreement, on eucharistic faith and practice, for unity" (II.49,52). The (Reformed) Church of Scotland judges "that while many differences in eucharistic interpretation and practice persist, for the most part they have the capacity neither to cause eucharistic separation nor to justify its perpetuation, and that the basis has been laid for full eucharistic communion" (I.86). Several Reformation and Free churches believe that the character of the eucharist as the supper of the Lord demands mutual reconciliation among the divided churches and eucharistic hospitality for those coming from other churches.

5. Conclusion

42. Listening to and analyzing the responses, we have discovered a broad agreement or convergence of many responses concerning the Trinitarian structure and meaning of the eucharist, the inseparability of word and sacrament, the "real, living and active presence" of Christ and the commemoration of his sacrifice, the mutual reference of *anamnesis*

---

[53] Anglican Church of the Southern Cone (I.59: "not a negotiable practice but a mistaken one"); Presbyterian Church in Ireland (III.214); Evangelical Church of Kurhessen-Waldeck, V.97; Uniting Church in Australia, IV.159.

and *epiklesis*, as well as the ethical, missionary and eschatological dimensions of the Lord's supper. Such agreement and convergence not only provide a framework for the settlement of remaining differences in eucharistic doctrine, but also suggest that the churches already share a largely common vision of the apostolic faith as a whole. A number of churches have already found sufficient agreement on the eucharist which has allowed them to enter into forms of eucharistic sharing. If other churches can pursue this agreement expressed in BEM and allow it to penetrate more and more into their understanding and life, there is cause for hope that the divisions among them will be overcome and they will be able to gather under the one word and celebrate as one *koinonia* with joy around the one table. May their continuing engagement with BEM contribute to that end. Glory be to God.

D. THE RESPONSES TO THE MINISTRY SECTION

1. Introduction

1. The section on ministry is the longest of the three sections of BEM. It is also divided up into more sub-sections and deals more descriptively and explicitly with a larger number of issues related to ministry. Because of its theme it is not only concerned with doctrinal questions and liturgical practice, like the other sections, but also with structures of the church. Consequently, the responses of the churches also contain, in general, longer parts on the ministry section of BEM than on the other sections. To summarize and evaluate in detail all this material would require a whole book. For the purpose of this report, therefore, it was only possible to refer to major issues and tendencies in the responses. The material contained in the responses is now available for other ecumenical studies and conversations and will be used in further Faith and Order work wherever appropriate.

2. For many, ecumenical dialogue on the ordained ministry poses some of the most difficult problems. This is also reflected in the style and presentation of the ministry section of BEM. It was expected, therefore, that the responses of the churches to this section would also be more critical than on the sections dealing with baptism and eucharist. Many churches have indeed come to such an evaluation and have stated so. A closer study of the responses, which was a presupposition of the summaries in this report, has revealed, however, that despite many critical comments on the general orientation of the text and on individual points,

a surprisingly large number of positive remarks on this section can be found in the responses of churches from all Christian traditions. This confirms the judgment that on the issue of the ministry also important ecumenical progress has been achieved over the last decades. This is an occasion for gratitude and hope.

2. The calling of the whole people of God (M.1-6)

3. The responses have unanimously welcomed M.1-6 of the ministry section, apart from some remarks on the wording of the text and the plea for introducing the perspective of "baptismal theology".[1] The responses affirm the approach of making the calling of the whole people of God the context for reflection on the ministry and many find an important ecclesiological statement here, firmly based on a sound Trinitarian theology. The United Methodist Church (USA) sees in this text "a superb retelling of the biblical history of God's saving work, extended beyond apostolic times to all history... This foundational narrative belongs to Christians of all generations and gives form and substance to every theory of ministry, lay or ordained" (II.193).

4. All churches seem to have appreciated the leading question of this section in M.6: "How, according to the will of God and under the guidance of the Holy Spirit, is the life of the Church to be understood and ordered, so that the Gospel may be spread and the community built up in love?"

5. This generally very positive reaction, however, leads to the disappointment expressed by quite a number of churches (especially Reformation) which observe that the inter-relation between the calling of the whole people of God and the service of the ordained ministry has not been sufficiently carried through in the rest of the ministry section. This critique is then also specified with regard to several paragraphs later in the text. A first attempt to take up this criticism in a positive way is made in "Clarifications", C.1, and in other elucidations of that part.

3. The church and the ordained ministry (M.8-14)

6. The vast majority of the responses have affirmed that the church, from its earliest existence and because of its missionary commitment, needs ministers, as described in M.8-13: persons ordained through the invocation of the Spirit and the laying on of hands (7c) and holding specific authority and responsibility (9), chosen and sent like the disciples

---

[1] Evangelical Lutheran Church in Bavaria, IV.34.

of Christ through the Holy Spirit (though they cannot repeat the unique role of the apostles insofar as they were witnesses to the resurrection of Christ). All responses with very few exceptions on minor points agree to the description of their tasks in biblical terms (11), their calling in and for the community (12) and the definition of their chief responsibility (13).

7. Some churches question the historical evidence about the role of the Twelve within the communities of the first generation (M.9 and 10)[2] or question the direct foundation of the ordained ministry (bishops) in the Twelve: "This form of reasoning from the twelve apostles to the first bishops requires us to leap from chronology to ontology of office and person."[3] But there are also those who would like to move into the opposite direction by stressing already in M.10 and 11 the idea of apostolic succession.[4]

8. Several churches express difficulties with the statement in M.8 that "the ministry of such persons, who since very early times have been ordained, is constitutive for the life and witness of the Church". They would prefer to consider the ministry as essential for the life of the church or (as a few indicate) as being part of its *bene esse* or well-being. This point is further considered in "Clarifications", C.2.

9. Similarly, the idea in M.8 that the ministers provide "a focus of its (the church's) unity" is regarded by some (Protestant) churches as contrary to their understanding which assigns this central position to Christ alone. This criticism is taken up in "Clarifications", C.3.

10. Critical comments were also provided by the formulation in M.11 that ordained ministers are *representatives* of Jesus Christ, and similarly in M.14 that Christ's presidency at the Lord's supper is signified and represented by an ordained minister. For some Orthodox responses this understanding leans too much in the direction of a functional understanding, while for them "the ministry is directly based on the will of Christ himself and founded by him and thus the bishop (or the priest) is the icon of Christ and not only his representative".[5] The Roman Catholic response regards representation as a valuable concept which needs, however, further qualification "so that through its relation to the Archetypos Christ,

---

[2] Church of the Province of New Zealand, II.67, and Religious Society of Friends (Quakers) in Great Britain, IV.222.
[3] United Church of Christ (USA), II.331.
[4] E.g., Inter-Orthodox Symposium of BEM, I.126.
[5] Finnish Orthodox Church, II.28. Similarly Russian Orthodox Church, II.9; Bulgarian Orthodox Church, II.21.

the ordained ministry is in and for the church an effective and sacramental reality, by which a minister acts 'in persona Christi'..." (VI.29). On the other side, for quite a number of responses from Reformation and Free churches, the concept of "representation" is either ambiguous or too narrowly linked with the ordained ministry. If one would speak of "representation" at all, this would be rather the task of all the members of the community or, as the United Church of Canada says, of the liturgy as a whole (II.282).

11. These different reactions have implications also for the presidency at the Lord's table (cf. last sentence of M.14). For the Orthodox, Roman Catholic, Old Catholic and Anglican responses this is necessarily reserved for an ordained minister. Most Lutheran and Reformed responses agree, in principle, with E.14, but several of these churches indicate that — on the basis of their understanding of the relation between eucharist and ordained ministry — there might be exceptions in situations where theologically trained ordained pastors are not available for pastoral and liturgical functions. Such exceptions are also — and more often — the case in Free churches. "Clarifications", C.4, provide some further comments on "representation".

4. Ordained ministry and authority (M.15-16)

12. With very few exceptions the responses welcome M.15 and 16 on the specific authority of the ordained ministry. "The section on 'ordained ministry and authority' contains two fine paragraphs on the manner and the spirit in which ordained ministers must exercise their authority with the co-operation of the whole community, focusing on the model of Christ himself and the way he revealed God's authority to the world."[6] The Orthodox Church in America adds that proper exercise of authority may sometimes involve confrontation, rebuke and correction expressed in preaching or penitential discipline (III.21) (similarly Lutheran Church in Australia [II.94] and Baptist Union of Sweden [IV.209]). Some Lutheran churches (Estonia, IV.44, Hanover, IV.53) cannot accept the thought that there is a special teaching authority conferred by God to ordained ministers.

13. This last comment is connected with the request of many churches that the issue of teaching authority in the church, which has not been taken up in BEM, together with the question of structures of decision-making and the participation of the laity in such structures (cf. also the

---

[6] Roman Catholic Church, VI. 29.

comments on M.27) should be taken up by Faith and Order in its future work. The ways in which the churches have prepared and adopted their responses to BEM would already provide important input into such a study.

5. Ordained ministry and priesthood (M.17)

14. For many responses this paragraph seems to be an acceptable bridge between different traditions and terminologies. The Orthodox and Roman Catholic responses, however, see a danger that the distinctive sacramental priesthood of the ordained ministers is put "side by side" with the priesthood of all believers.[7] On the other side of the spectrum of responses a number of churches suggest avoiding the title "priest" because it could be seen as prejudging the unique priesthood of Christ and the priesthood of all believers.[8]

15. The commentary to M.17 is praised by most responses for its clarification of the biblical and historical evidence. The Roman Catholic response adds that "the reality of 'sacrifice', mentioned explicitly for Christ and the priesthood of the baptized, is absent, although it belongs inherently to the concept of ordained priesthood. Certain ministers are called priests because of their specific part in presiding at the celebration of the eucharist, as 'heralds and ambassadors' of Christ, who gives himself as sacrifice for all" (VI.30).[9] On the issue of priesthood cf. "Clarifications", C.5.

6. The ministry of men and women in the church (M.18)

16. While most responses affirm the need, expressed in M.18, that women and men must find their appropriate place and responsibilities in the life of the churches, they share in different ways and for different reasons the disappointment of the Church of Christ in Thailand: "... we feel that the part related to ordained women is too brief and touches only the surface" (V.174). Thus, the existing divisions over this issue (described in the commentary to M.18) are clearly expressed in the responses. A number of churches which ordain women regret that BEM has not come forward with a more positive stance towards this position

---

[7] Bulgarian Orthodox Church, II.21; Finnish Orthodox Church, II.27; Roman Catholic Church, VI.30.

[8] E.g., Mar Thoma Syrian Church of Malabar, IV.12; Presbyterian Church in Wales, II.172; Methodist Church in Ireland, II.234.

[9] See also Church of England, III.58f.

and some miss a reference to gender in M.50 which, according to the Burma Baptist Convention, "seems to evade the question of women's ordination" (IV.189). They affirm that the "willingness to ordain women is required if we are to remain faithful to our understanding of the gospel"[10] or similarly: "Our commitment to the ordination of women is an integral part of our obedience to the Gospel",[11] "the ordination of women is a faithful expression of the apostolic tradition",[12] "we see the ministry of women as a gift to the church from the Holy Spirit",[13] "a positive good and appropriate to the human expression of the fullness of Christ's priesthood in the Church".[14] From such positions follows the conclusion that "we cannot allow any prospect that ordination of women could be given up for the sake of church unity".[15]

17. From the side of churches which do not ordain women, M.18 is criticized for showing "a clear tendency to solve the problem favourably"[16] and for the fact "that BEM has not adequately summarized the weighty biblical and theological arguments against the ordination of women, nor does it recognize what serious barriers these are to full doctrinal unity".[17] The Roman Catholic response, however, approves of "the nuanced way in which the 'ministry of men and women in the Church' is treated. We recognize fully that the experience of the churches which practise the ordination of women constitutes inevitably a challenge to our own position... Even if differences on these issues can raise obstacles to recognition of certain ministries, they should never become prejudiced to further reflection upon the ordained ministry within the ecumenical context" (VI.30). Here also, the reference to tradition in the commentary to M.18 is strengthened by "we have no authority to change" the tradition of the church *(ibid)*. The Orthodox responses state their position which does not allow for the ordination of women to the priesthood, but they also stress the need for further participation of

---

[10] United Methodist Church (USA), II.195.
[11] Lutheran Church in America, I.35.
[12] Presbyterian Church (USA), III.200f.
[13] Disciples of Christ, I.120.
[14] Episcopal Church (USA), II.60. The Old Catholic Church in Austria (mimeo) refers to the findings of the International Conference of Old Catholic Theologians according to which there are "neither biblical nor theological reasons which speak against women in the priesthood".
[15] United Methodist Church (USA), II.195.
[16] Russian Orthodox Church, II.9.f.
[17] Lutheran Church-Missouri Synod, III.141.

women at all levels of church life except those which are reserved for the ordained ministry.[18] The Romanian Orthodox Church also notes that the question of mutual recognition of ordained ministries in relation to the question of churches also ordaining women and the question concerning the methods of achieving union "could get competent answers only by joint decision of all Orthodox churches" (III.12). The problems and conflicts raised by this question within and among Anglican churches are expressed, e.g., in the response of the Scottish Episcopal Church (II.50).

The Federation of Evangelical Churches in the GDR underlines that the decision of each church on this issue "should be respected by other churches in such a way that it does not present any obstacles for the mutual recognition of ministries (M.54)" (V.145).

18. It is obvious that this difficult issue requires further discussion in Faith and Order — most probably in the wider context of ecclesiology and the role and place of women in the diverse ministries and functions in the church. For further comment cf. "Clarifications", C.6.

7. The forms of the ordained ministry (M.19-25)

19. In general there is an affirmation of this part of the ministry section. A large number of responses endorse the opening statement of M.19: "The New Testament does not describe a single pattern of ministry which might serve as a blueprint or continuing norm for all future ministry in the Church." The Romanian Orthodox Church states, however, that "the structures of ordained ministry are wanted and instituted by Christ himself" (III.11). There is likewise considerable appreciation for the description of the development of the threefold pattern of bishop, presbyter and deacon in M.19-22, for the recognition in M.24 of the evident need of its reform and for the need of a ministry of episkope (M.23). Churches with the traditional episcopal structure welcome the plea for the restoration of the threefold pattern for the sake of unity (M.22). A number of other churches express willingness to reflect on this proposal with the indication that the respective functions are often present even where this pattern and the titles are formally absent.[19] Those who are open to considering the threefold pattern as a basis for unity propose, however,

---

[18] Russian Orthodox Church, II.10; Romanian Orthdox Church III.13; Orthodox Church in America, III.24f.; Malankara Syrian Orthodox Church, V.5 (referring to women saints as equal intercessors in the church).

[19] E.g., Evangelical Church of the Czech Brethren, IV.116; Evangelical Church of Westphalia, IV.146f.

several reforms concerning the relation between bishops, presbyters and deacons, their relationship to the participation of laity, their collegiality and integration into synodical structures.[20]

20. But there are also many responses from the Reformation and Free churches which, while not necessarily rejecting the threefold pattern in principle, especially if it is not understood in a hierarchical sense, reject or at least question the normative character of the threefold pattern: "... a unified structuring of a threefold ministry can well have a practical mission and thereby advance the unity of the churches, but not that it is necessary for unity".[21] They find that the scriptural diversity, mentioned in M.19, should be kept throughout history: "Since in the first century the variety of ministries did not call into question the unity of the church, the different forms of the ministry should not be allowed to become a source of division among the churches of the present day," states the Evangelical Church of the Congo (V.168). These responses also find that the case for the threefold pattern is overstated on the basis of a historical development (and they raise in this connection the question of Scripture and Tradition), that this pattern as such did not — as history shows — guarantee unity and that other patterns — like the fourfold pattern of the presbyterial system of Calvin or the idea of one ordained ministry in the Lutheran tradition — might serve unity as well.

For a number of churches from this group it would be possible to consider this threefold pattern if it were kept on the level of human design and order and not of divine order *(de iure divino).*[22] "We acknowledge that the threefold office of ministry does draw our attention to indispensable functions in the church; BEM has again let us see this afresh. We should however like to remain free to redesignate these *functions* responsibly as ministries of the church in the service of the gospel and the community."[23] The issue of the threefold pattern is taken up in "Clarifications", C.7.

21. "We recognize in the Presbyterian Church in Cameroon the one ordained ministry of the pastor" (I.82). Also many Lutheran churches

---

[20] E.g., Uniting Church in Australia, IV.163f.; Burma Baptist Convention, IV.189; North Elbian Evangelical Lutheran Church, I.48-50; Old Catholic Church of Switzerland, V.14f.; Federation of Evangelical Churches in the GDR, V.140-142 (should be studied in depth).
[21] Church of Sweden, II.138.
[22] E.g., Evangelical Lutheran Church of Iceland, IV.67; Evangelical Church of the Augsburg Confession in Romania, IV.89f.; Evangelical Church in Baden, V.52.
[23] Swiss Protestant Church Federation, VI.79.

echo this conviction that there is *only one ordained* ministry which might, however, be exercised in different forms, on different levels and under different titles.[24] This issue is taken up in "Clarifications", C.7. And there is the reminder that this one ministry, which can be exercised in many different contexts and together with other non-ordained forms of ministry, is characterized by the tension between its priestly and prophetic function, that it is not only serving the building up of the community but also the church's mission in the world.[25]

8. Guiding principles for the exercise of the ordained ministry in the church (M.26-27)

22. Most of the responses have endorsed the statements in this part of the text. They also see in them challenges to the ways in which the exercise of ministry and the structures guiding this exercise are ordered in their own churches. Quite a number of responses from Reformation and Free churches, however, question whether the recommendation of Lausanne 1927, quoted in the commentary of M.26, has been applied throughout the ministry section of BEM.[26] In general, these churches miss in this and in other parts of the ministry section adequate attention to the *presbyterial-synodical* structures of ministerial and church order.[27] Some indicate that the concept of *collegiality* should also embrace the common ministry of ordained and non-ordained[28] and several episcopal churches (especially Anglican in Australia, Canada and New Zealand) plead for the inclusion of lay people in the synods of the church. Finally, a number of churches miss a consideration of the *local and universal* dimensions of the church not only in the ministry section, but in all three sections of BEM.[29] In this context the omission of the question of the *primacy* of patriarchs and/or the universal ministry of the bishop of Rome is seen by some as a serious shortcoming of the text.[30]

---

[24] E.g., Evangelical Lutheran Church of Canada, II.103; Churches of Norway, II.119, Sweden, II.138, and Finland, III.123; Evangelical Lutheran Church in Bavaria, IV.38.
[25] Church of South India, II.78.
[26] E.g., Church of Scotland, I.96; Evangelical Lutheran Church in Oldenburg, VI.79; Reformed Churches in the Netherlands, VI.107.
[27] E.g., Episcopal Church (USA), II.60; Presbyterian Church of Canada, II.157; Evangelical Reformed Church in North-West Germany, IV.98.
[28] Federation of Evangelical Churches in the GDR, V.140.
[29] E.g., Old Catholic Churches in Switzerland (V.9) and in Germany (mimeographed document); Episcopal Church, USA, II.60; Church of England, III.36.
[30] E.g., Evangelical Church of the Augsburg Confession of Alsace and Lorraine, III.157.

23. For these questions on collegiality, synodal structures and primacy cf. also "Clarifications", C.9.

9. Functions of bishops, presbyters and deacons (M.28-31)

24. Reactions to the descriptions of the functions of these ministries vary. Some responses seem to see no problem here: "While we are able broadly to endorse the descriptions of the tasks... we would have to reject unambiguously any interpretation of the inter-relationship of the three ministries in a hierarchical sense."[31] Quite a number take up the question of the diaconate. They welcome the broader description of this ministry and the impulse of BEM to further reflection on the forms of the diaconate which they have preserved or reintroduced (or are open to reintroduce), but some of them also note that in their own structure deacons are not seen as sharing in the ordained ministry.[32] Cf. also "Clarifications", C.7.

25. As mentioned already in relation to M.23, the concept of episkope is taken up by many responses and is then also considered in relation to the functions of bishops. A number of responses ask for a clarification of the relation between episkope and episcopacy (cf. "Clarifications", C.8). Reformation and Free churches express a "functional" understanding of episkope[33] while the Roman Catholic and Orthodox churches emphasize that "it is more than a function of oversight next to other functions and ministries"; it is also "a sacramental sign of integration and a focus of communion".[34] Though they are prepared to widen the meaning and function of episkope, they still value episcopacy as the supreme and indispensable sacramental form of such episkope.

10. Succession in the apostolic tradition (M.34-38)

26. The distinction (not separation) between "apostolic Tradition" and "succession of the Apostolic ministry" in M.34-38 has been widely accepted in the responses as an important ecumenical step forward in the difficult issue of "apostolic succession": "We are grateful for the theological reflection stimulated by the section on apostolic tradition and succes-

---

[31] North Elbian Evangelical Lutheran Church, I.50.
[32] E.g., Evangelical Churches of Hessen-Nassau, IV.136, and in Kurhessen-Waldeck, V.100; Church of the Czech Brethren, IV.117.
[33] E.g., Church of Scotland, I.86f. and 92; Church of Norway, II.120; Reformed Church of America, II.149f.
[34] Roman Catholic Church, VI.33; Russian Orthodox Church, II.9; Finnish Orthodox Church, II.28; Romanian Orthodox Church, III.13; Orthodox Church of America, III.20 and 23; cf. also Church of England, III.57 and 77.

sion."[35] The Church of North India "commends the broad interpretation of apostolic succession in BEM as a helpful approach to bringing the so-called episcopal and non-episcopal churches closer to each other without denying their own heritage" (II.73). But there is also the impression of the Bulgarian Orthodox Church (and other Orthodox churches): "Obviously here we have divided two things that are inextricably bound up: the apostolic tradition and the apostolic ministry."[36] Also the suggestion to recognize other forms of an orderly transmission of ministry and, at the same time, to recognize the limits of episcopal succession as not automatically guaranteeing continuity and unity seems to go too far for the Roman Catholic and Orthodox responses, which emphasize that the character of episcopal succession as a guarantee and "effective sign" must be safeguarded as a condition for unity and recognition of ministry.[37]

27. The response of the Church of Norway seems to articulate the position of many Reformation and Free churches: "The matter of succession ought therefore, first and foremost, to serve as a call to continuous reflection on the apostolic integrity and doctrinal continuity of the church. We cannot see that the validity of ministerial acts performed by ordained persons is dependent on being able to trace back to the first apostles a formal succession of the laying on of hands" (II.121). Such a position does not, however, exclude an openness towards the apostolic succession, which "we could perfectly well assume as a visible sign of the mutual recognition of one another's principal offices of ministry, even if it is not on our side a presupposition for such recognition".[38] On this matter of succession, which remains a major issue for further dialogue "on whether or how the sign of episcopal succession can be recovered (M.38) in a way which does not in fact throw the existing continuity with apostolic faith, worship and mission into question",[39] cf. also "Clarifications", C.11.

11. Ordination (M.39-50)

28. All responses to BEM which affirm that the churches must have a ministry, as described in M.13, accept the need for a specific act of

---

[35] American Lutheran Church, II.83; Roman Catholic Church IV.32f. and others.
[36] II.22f.; Finnish Orthodox Church, II.28f.; Russian Orthodox Church, II.9.
[37] Roman Catholic Church, IV.32f.; Russian Orthodox Church, II.7; Romanian Orthodox Church, III.13; Orthodox Church in America, III.23.
[38] Church of Denmark, III.114; cf. also Evangelical Church of Berlin-Brandenburg (West Berlin), VI.67.
[39] United Reformed Church in the UK, I.108.

ordination. With very few exceptions they have also generally endorsed the description and theological interpretation of that act in M.39-44. For example, the Federation of Evangelical Churches in the GDR affirms: "In the account given of the meaning of ordination (M.39ff.) we recognize the essentials of the understanding of ordination in the tradition fashioned by the Reformation (with *vocatio, benedictio, missio*)" (V.144). The vast majority of responses agree that the ordination of those called by God to the church's ministries is both an action of God and of the church which should include an invocation of the Holy Spirit and the laying on of hands. Several churches underline a pneumatological understanding of ordination,[40] and a response from Korea notes that the reference to the community and to collegiality "keeps some of the Korean church's revivalists from using it (i.e. ordination) superstitiously".[41] An open question for several churches is: which ministries require ordination? Reformed churches, e.g., recognize uncertainty about the functions of presbyters (elders) and deacons: whether they should be ordained or not.[42]

29. The main problem for Reformation and Free churches in this connection is the tendency towards a sacramental understanding of ordination (especially in M.41 and 43) which they cannot accept or which should at least be further clarified.[43] "When ordination is described as 'sacramental sign' (M.41)", states the Evangelical Lutheran Church in Bavaria, "we understand this in the sense that the ordained is made aware through a visible event of God's promise applying to him. However, theological clarification is necessary on this point which must be connected with a reflection on the understanding of the sacrament" (IV.40). The responses of the Orthodox churches note that BEM is not clear enough about the essential view of ordination (and ministry in general) as a sacramental reality.[44] The Roman Catholic response states that "the text describes the act of ordination in a way consonant with the faith and the practice of the Catholic Church" (VI.33) and "meets in many ways the Catholic concept of ordination as a sacrament" (VI.34). But it should

---

[40] E.g., Presbyterian Church in Cameroon, I.82.
[41] Presbyterian Church of Korea, II.164.
[42] E.g., Church of Scotland I.96; Churches of Christ in Australia II.273.
[43] E.g., American Lutheran Church, II.83; Baptist Union of Great Britain and Ireland, I.77; Presbyterian Church of Canada, II.158.
[44] Bulgarian Orthodox Church, II.22; Romanian Orthodox Church, III.10 and 13; Orthodox Church in America, III.22f. Similarly the (Anglican) Church of Melanesia: "There seems to be a complete silence on the sacramental aspects and sacramental function of the ordained ministry", III.97.

have been stated clearly that "ordination is not only a sign, but an effective sign" and "that ordination is indeed a sacrament" (VI.34). The issue of a sacramental understanding of ordination has been taken up in "Clarifications", C.12.

12. Towards the mutual recognition of the ordained ministries (M.51-55)

30. Not too many churches have specifically reacted to this concluding part of the ministry section of BEM dealing with steps towards mutual recognition of ministries. The responses clearly reveal different positions on this issue. On the one hand, there are many churches of the Reformation and Free church tradition which show a willingness to recognize the ministries of other churches including "episcopal" churches. The openness of Anglican churches at this point is expressed in the challenge: "In view of the Lima statement, especially M.28, the Church of the Province of South Africa needs seriously to consider ways in which it can recognize ministries of other churches without a ceremony which may seem to imply reordination."[45] A number of the responses from Reformation and Free churches, however, criticize what they regard as an imbalance between the steps proposed in M.53(a) and (b) because they are requested to take a structural step in M.53(b (entering the episcopal succcession) while the "episcopal" churches are merely asked to make an act of recognition.

31. The Roman Catholic and Orthodox churches are not ready to move towards such an act of recognition of ministries in "non-episcopal" churches: "... we believe that ordained ministries require sacramental ordination by a bishop standing in the apostolic succession. We hope that a growing fraternal solidarity of collaboration, common reflection, prayer and service between churches and ecclesial communities, and particularly their ministries, can reach a point of seeing whether, or in what terms, an ordained ministry recognized by all might become possible."[46] The Orthodox churches refuse likewise (explicitly or implicitly) to accept the suggestions in M.53.[47] Yet they indicate in various ways that this does not close the issue: "The fundamental ecclesiological problem of unity lies not in an 'ecumenical' mutual recognition of 'ministry', but in recognition of the church, in which this ministry is exercised, as a 'true church'

---

[45] Church of the Province of South Africa, II.104.
[46] Roman Catholic Church, VI.35.
[47] Russian Orthodox Church, II.9; Bulgarian Orthodox Church, II.23; Finnish Orthodox Church, II.28; Romanian Orthodox Church, III.11; Orthodox Church in America, III.23f.

confessing the faith of the apostles."[48] Similarly the Roman Catholic response says: "It must be clear that the recognition of ordained ministry cannot be isolated from its ecclesiological context. The recognition of the ordained ministry and of the ecclesial character of a Christian community are indissolubly and mutually related" (VI.36). Also Reformation and Free churches can agree with such a perspective, and here lies a possible way forward in the framework of a common reflection on the understanding of the church as indicated in "Clarifications", C.13.

13. Concluding considerations

32. In the preceding summaries major lines of affirmation and important critical reactions in the responses to the ministry section of BEM have been indicated. These should be read together with the "Clarifications", where an attempt has been made to listen to and take up some of the most frequent critical comments and thus open the way for continuing the dialogue.

33. In these concluding remarks we would like, in a very preliminary way, to point to some conclusions which might be drawn from the rich material in the responses:

a) One of the most important ecumenical convergences seems to be the recognition, expressed in many responses, that a common understanding of the nature of the church and of the sacraments of baptism and the eucharist is fundamental for any theology and structure of ministry and for mutual recognition of ministries — and not the reverse.

b) Many seem to agree that mutual recognition of baptism and the Lord's supper is a basic ecclesiological reality which signifies and manifests the already given unity and should, finally, lead to the recognition of a true ecclesial character and of ministry in other churches.[49]

c) The calling of the whole people of God as a basic ecclesiological perspective for an ecumenical understanding of ministry has been favourably noted by the responses, even though there are clear warnings not to consider the ordained ministry as a simple derivation of this general New Testament typology of the church. Such common ecclesiological perspectives have positive consequences for an ecumenical vision of ministry and should, therefore, be further developed.

---

[48] Russian Orthodox Church, II.9.
[49] E.g., Greek Orthodox Patriarchate of Alexandria, III.1; Roman Catholic Church, VI.38-40; Anglican Church of Canada, II.40; Church of England, III.34,36f.,41; Estonian Lutheran Church, IV.43; Netherlands Reformed Church/Reformed Churches in the Netherlands, IV.103; Federation of Evangelical Churches in the GDR, V.122.

d) The distinction made in BEM between what is constitutive or essential and time-bound or contextual with regard to the ministry has been welcomed by many responses. "An ecumenical discernment is needed to see what belongs to the constitutive structure of the church and what to the contingent social organization."[50] The same judgment is expressed in the request of many responses of Reformation and Free churches to clarify on what aspects of the understanding and forms of the ministry an agreement is necessary and where a diversity is legitimate.

e) A considerable number of responses indicate the ways in which BEM is calling their churches to fresh reflections on their understanding and forms of ministry. In addition many have obviously also been encouraged by BEM to reflect in different ways and with different suggestions on the forms of ministry, their renewal and reform in view of new situations and challenges, the introduction of new ministries, appropriate ways of their personal, collegial and communal exercise and adequate forms of inter-relation and co-operation between ordained ministries and other ministries and lay persons in the church. This is described in *section E of this chapter*.

f) The considerable material available in the responses which deals with the concerns mentioned under (e), but also all the other reflections and comments, provides ample opportunity for the churches to learn from the insights and experiences of others. This opportunity has been welcomed by many responses. "Our hope is that the responses of sister churches to the text will help us to understand both the strengths and the weaknesses of our ministry as we have not done before."[51]

g) We conclude from the responses that the deepest differences between the churches concerning mutual recognition of ministries relate to the issues of the ordination of women and episcopal succession. Ecumenical dialogue on these issues will have to continue between the churches and in Faith and Order. This might best be done within the framework of more comprehensive ecumenical reflection on ecclesiology, as has been suggested by the response of the Ecumenical Patriarchate of Constantinople and by several other churches: "... we would express the view and the hope that ecclesiology will be among the immediate priority in the programmes of the Commission on Faith and Order during the coming years, closely linked to the three sacraments *(mysteria)* of baptism, eucharist and ministry" (IV.5).

---

[50] Roman Catholic Church, VI.31.
[51] Methodist Church (Great Britain), II.227.

E. THE RESPONSES TO THE QUESTIONS IN THE PREFACE

1. Introduction

1. The four questions in the preface to *Baptism, Eucharist and Ministry (BEM)* seemed to have fulfilled their purpose. They have challenged and helped the churches not only to evaluate the content of BEM but also to clarify and formulate implications of this document for their own faith and life and for their ecumenical relations. In many responses to BEM the four questions have been either:
— used to structure the whole response;
— integrated into the comments on the three sections of BEM;
— presented in the form of a concluding summary;
— implicitly operative in the way a response has been formulated.

Taken all together several hundred pages in the six-volume documentation *Churches Respond to BEM* refer directly to the four questions. Consequently, only a summary of aspects and general tendencies from this rich material can be presented here.

2. This summary will not include the responses to the *first question: "the extent to which your church can recognize in this text the faith of the Church through the ages"*. These responses have been taken up in part A of this chapter (paras 30-34), in the description of the comments on the three sections of BEM in this chapter and in chapter V. "Major Issues", A. Scripture and Tradition.

2. Responses to the second question

3. In the *second question* from the preface to BEM the churches were asked to indicate *"the consequences your church can draw from this text for its relations and dialogues with other churches, particularly with those churches which also recognize the text as an expression of the apostolic faith"*. In part A of this chapter (paras 16 and 17) some general directions in explicit or implicit reactions to this question have already been mentioned. It is also obvious that there is a close interrelation between questions two and three. Relations and dialogues with other churches will lead to changes in theology and practice of the churches involved, while such changes in turn are a presupposition for progress in ecumenical relations and dialogues. Accordingly, several responses have made comments with regard to the second question which could have been made as a reaction to the third question, and vice versa.

4. Many responses consider the Lima document as a good basis and instrument for improved *ecumenical relations*, better *mutual understanding* and *sharing between the churches*. Accordingly, the Church of Jesus Christ in Madagascar testifies that "the BEM text has brought about a lessening of the conflicts which formerly existed in Madagascar between Christians of the various churches, especially between Protestants and Catholics. BEM has facilitated local, regional and national relations between the different churches and has contributed to the progress of ecumenism in Madagascar. BEM has encouraged Christians' enthusiasm for collaboration to improve and consolidate points of agreement and for a joint quest in search of solutions to what still divides them" (III.187).[1] The new possibilities for mutual exchange and sharing are indicated by the United Church of Christ, USA: "The convergence in the text, though by no means complete, affords us a clarity of focus that challenges us to share more generously the ecclesial gifts that we have come to cherish, and to cherish more graciously the ecclesial gifts offered to us by other churches" (II.334).

5. The responses of non-sacramental communions, which express "fears regarding the exclusion from this fellowship of churches" as a "consequence of taking the Lima text literally", nevertheless affirm that "the study has enabled us to appreciate in a new way the richness of the traditions of our sister churches" (The Salvation Army, IV.254-255). And the Religious Society of Friends in Great Britain, which has published its response under the title "To Lima With Love", sees its contribution to dialogue and mutual sharing in the testimony: "Over more than 300 years we have witnessed to a redemptive religious experience. Though this has been without baptism, eucharist or ministry in the traditional senses, it has been a consequence of personal and repentant response and corporate worship in the context of silent, receptive waiting upon God" (IV.225).

6. Many churches draw from BEM the conclusion that BEM should be used as an encouragement, resource and framework for ongoing or new *ecumenical dialogues* — multilateral and especially also bilateral. The Anglican Church of Canada is quite specific in this respect: "Dialogues have already been enriched by the joint study of BEM. The Anglican-Roman Catholic dialogue in Canada has an ongoing working group studying BEM. The United Church-Anglican Task Force on the Mutual Recognition of Ordained Ministry found support for its work in the ministry section. BEM has been a focus of discussion for interchurch

---

[1] Cf. also, e.g., Moravian Church in Jamaica, V.172; Presbyterian Church in Cameroon, I.83; Melanesian Council of Churches, V.185.

dialogue groups across the country on the local level; indeed, in some areas it has been the motivation of the establishment of serious interchurch study for the first time" (II.40). The Lutheran Church in America regards BEM as a "resource in differing ways for Lutherans in their dialogues with Anglican, Orthodox, Reformed and Roman Catholic traditions. It gives Lutherans all the more reason to be involved in multilateral dialogues and bilateral dialogues, showing how both belong together" (I.36). The Church of Scotland considers one of the uses of BEM in the coming years to be "a frame of reference for interchurch conversations... in that on the one hand it shows established agreements and convergences (and thus prevents misunderstandings and unnecessary controversies), and on the other hand it shows areas of difference or obscurity or calling in some way for further exploration; above all it distinguishes clearly between differences that divide and differences that do not or need not divide" (I.89).[2] Finally, the Roman Catholic Church adds the reminder that "theological dialogue must not be isolated from other ecumenical efforts to break down barriers between Christians" (VI.36).

7. The significance of the convergences in the understanding and practice of *baptism* for ecumenical relations is taken up in many responses. Many of them, like the Church of Norway, start from "the fundamental idea that baptism in essence is one, and that it is... a being grafted into the body of Christ, and thereby is actually the primary bond of unity in the church. In the profoundest sense there is only one baptism" (II.110). The report of the National Council of Churches in the Philippines, which itself is the result of a concrete response to the second question in the form of a dialogue on the baptism section of BEM, considers some possible conclusions: "Baptism is generally agreed to be incorporation into the body of Christ which is the church. This church is the universal church whose membership is made up of all those who believe in Jesus Christ as the Lord and Saviour. This universal church is visible in particular situations in the form of the local church. The question therefore arises, does baptism in one

---

[2] The importance of BEM for ecumenical dialogue is also underlined by, e.g., the Ecumenical Patriarchate, IV.3, and the Orthodox Churches in Finland, II.29, and Romania, III.14; Melanesian Council of Churches, V.185; Episcopal Church, USA, II.61; Southern and Northern Provinces of the Moravian Church in America, II.258 and 262; Methodist Church, GB, II.214; Lutheran Churches in Oldenburg, IV.74, Canada, II.104, and Hungary, III.130; Evangelical Church of Westphalia, IV.149-150, which outlines several stages of recognition and fellowship.

local church entitle one to membership in another local church which practises a different form of baptism?" (V.190).

8. This leads on to the conviction expressed by the Church of England, that BEM "asks Baptists to acknowledge that those churches, where by very ancient tradition indeed infants are admitted to the sacrament, are validly and effectively receiving them into the Church of Christ. This is a sensitive and difficult matter but any future bilateral conversation must consider whether the theological convergences in the Lima text, especially the emphasis on initiation as a process, means that the two baptismal practices can be contained within a truly united church" (III.67). The Burma Baptist Convention, e.g., took up the challenge, noted that "a convergence has taken place" and, on the basis of its own understanding of baptism as a process of initiation, expressed the view that a *"mutual recognition of baptism has become a possibility"* (italics in the text) (IV.187). Quite a number of churches already recognize baptisms in other churches (usually with certain conditions) or express their readiness to recognize the baptism in churches "which likewise recognize the convergence statement as an expression of the apostolic faith".[3] And this is already happening: "The consequence of the BEM text here in Madagascar has been to confirm 'mutual recognition of baptism'," reports the Church of Jesus Christ in Madagascar (III.187).

9. Many churches draw positive conclusions for their ongoing and future dialogues[4] and their ecumenical relations also from the section on the *eucharist*. These, however, are more differentiated. Thus, the Scottish Episcopal Church "recognizes the second part (on Eucharist) of this report as sufficient agreement, on eucharistic faith and practice, for unity" (II.52).[5] The Presbyterian Church, USA, draws a concrete conclusion from such recognition: "The increased mutual understanding expressed in the text encourages us in intercommunion and in the development and use of common liturgies and ecumenical liturgies (e.g., the COCU liturgy and the Lima liturgy)" (III.196). Also Lutheran and United churches refer to

---

[3] Federation of Evangelical Churches in the GDR, V.148; some few other examples: Evangelical Church of the Augsburg Confession, Romania, IV.83; Evangelical Church in Hesse and Nassau, IV.130; North Elbian Evangelical Lutheran Church, I.42; United Reformed Church in the United Kingdom, I.106; Anglican Church of Canada, II.40; Methodist Church, GB, II.214; United Protestant Church of Belgium, III.168-169; Presbyterian Church, USA, III.191.

[4] Cf., e.g., United Methodist Church, USA, II.190.

[5] Other Anglican churches describe existing forms of eucharistic sharing (Anglican Church of Canada, II.41) or regulations for it (Church of England, III.68-69).

their practice of or readiness, on the basis of BEM, for forms of eucharistic hospitality or sharing,[6] and the Church of England clarifies conditions for joint celebrations of the Lord's supper (III.69-70).

10. The Federation of Evangelical Churches in the GDR indicates several stages: "With those churches which also recognize the convergence text on the eucharist as attesting the Christian, apostolic faith, our church would like to hold conversations, with a view to mutual recognition of the celebration of the eucharist and, ultimately, intercommunion and intercelebration. In regard to churches for which such recognition is still impossible we are ready for our part, as a first step in that direction, to offer and receive eucharistic hospitality... In the light of our understanding of the Lord's supper, according to which it is Christ who invites us to the table and offers himself and his salvation to all members of his community who seek him, eucharistic hospitality is in principle possible" (V.148-149). These churches are, however, aware that for some churches further conditions like an agreement on the ministry and on the apostolic faith in all its fundamental points must be fulfilled before forms of eucharistic sharing are possible as an expression of unity among them.[7]

11. The responses to the Lima document reveal once again that for Reformation and Free churches mutual recognition of *ministries*, given certain conditions, presents no major problem, while in a broader ecumenical perspective this issue still presents the greatest difficulties for ecumenical advance. Representative for the group of churches mentioned above[8] is the statement of the North Elbian Evangelical Lutheran Church: "On the basis of its confession of faith (CA.7), our church has no grounds for refusing to recognize the *ordained ministry of other churches* where this ministry clearly serves the pure proclamation of the gospel and the administration of the sacraments in accordance with Christ's institution. But if the way to church fellowship is not to be blocked, our church, too, is bound to require from other churches a full recognition of its ordained

---

[6] Cf., e.g., Lutheran Churches of Iceland, IV.63, Denmark, III.112, Romania, IV.86, Brunswick, VI.47, North Elbia, I.47, Norway, II.116, and Sweden, II.133; Evangelical Churches of Hesse-Nassau, IV.133, Westphalia, IV.149, and Kurhessen-Waldeck, V.97; Church of North India, II.69; Mission Covenant Church of Sweden, II.319.

[7] Cf. Roman Catholic Church, VI.38, which, however, regards a reception of the basic convergences in the eucharist section as "an important development" and as "a new level in regard to achieving common faith on the eucharist".

[8] C.f., e.g., Estonian Evangelical Lutheran Church, IV.46; Evangelical Lutheran Church in Württemberg, V.31; Federation of Evangelical Churches in the GDR, V.149; Presbyterian Church, USA, III.201-202; United Protestant Church of Belgium, III.177.

ministry, which in its case is exercised by both men and women" (I.51). Several responses express the readiness to reconsider aspects of the ministry in the light of BEM in terms both of the renewal of the life of the respective churches and of preparing the way towards mutual recognition.[9] The ecumenical implications of the issue of the ordination of women are referred to in part D of this chapter and in chapter IV, "Clarifications", C.6.

12. Anglican churches seem to move towards forms of recognition. Thus, the Church of the Province of Southern Africa mentions a number of points for further clarification and concludes: "In view of the Lima statement, especially M.28, the CPSA needs seriously to consider ways in which it can recognize ministries of other churches without a ceremony which may seem to imply reordination. The CPSA needs to consider the possibility of recognizing the orders of women ministers and the obstacles to union which they appear to constitute" (III.104). The Church of England believes that questions relating to the recognition of ministries and their eventual reconciliation "must be set within a wider ecclesiological framework" (III.71), and the Scottish Episcopal Church suggests that on the basis of an "agreement on the form of the united church, it will be easier to work out how to integrate the ordained ministry in the course of moving out of separation into unity" (II.52). For the Roman Catholic Church "it is not only agreement on the question of apostolic succession, but also being situated within it, that is necessary for recognition of ordination". But there are steps towards this goal. If, for example, "the threefold ministry of bishop, presbyter and deacon, explained in BEM, were adopted generally by Christian communities, that would put the churches and ecclesial communities on a new level of relationship... There are already grounds on which mutual respect can begin to grow and dimensions of fellowship between our communions can be built, reflecting the levels of communion that now exist" (VI.38-39).

3. Responses to the third question

13. In the *third question* from the preface to BEM the churches were asked to indicate *"the guidance your church can take from this text for its worship, educational, ethical and spiritual life and witness"*. In part A of this chapter (paras 13-15) reference has already been made to more general statements which respond to this question, and also the descrip-

---

[9] In relation to the threefold pattern of ministry, cf. e.g., Evangelical Church of the Augsburg Confession, Romania, IV.89-90; United Methodist Church, USA, II.194-196.

tion of the comments on the three sections of BEM contain material which corresponds directly or indirectly to the intention of this question. Because of the richness of the material again only a few responses can be quoted and major common concerns indicated. A number of responses combine reaction to BEM and reflection on faith and practice throughout the whole text without specifically referring to the third question.[10]

14. Several responses list major implications for their *own faith and life*. For example, the Waldensian and Methodist churches in Italy refer to their worship, life, witness, instruction, ethics and spirituality, where (for spirituality) the Lima document "can be an instrument for the reciprocal enrichment that can come to us through contact with the richness of the Lord's gifts and expressions of piety that the Spirit has given to the various churches" (II.253). The Church of North India lists especially catechesis and worship: "(a) In catechesis the text can become the basis of teaching, discussions and preaching. This will not only lead our congregations into a deeper understanding of their faith, but will also bring them closer to Christians of other denominations. (b) The Lima liturgy can be celebrated in intrachurch as well as interchurch situations" (II.69). Those two aspects, which are emphasized in many responses,[11] are further specified by the Christian Church (Disciples of Christ) by proposing, that "BEM be used in such areas as the development of church school curricula, material for membership classes and lay study groups, teaching in theological seminaries, providing direction for the work of regional commissions on ministry, and the ongoing work of the Council on Christian Unity. Secondly, BEM offers help as Disciples enrich their worship through liturgical renewal. BEM will come to life for Disciples by its use in the development of services, celebrations, and orders of worship, and in our teaching the meaning of baptism, eucharist and ministry" (I.120).

15. The Evangelical Church of the Augsburg Confession of Alsace and Lorraine affirms that "the Lima document prompts us to reconsider our baptismal and eucharistic liturgies and to update them by making full use of the wealth of the universal tradition. It also invites us to re-examine our

---

[10] E.g., the Presbyterian Churches in Ghana, VI.88ff., Cameroon, I.83-84, Canada, II.152ff., and Korea, II.160ff.; Christian Church (Disciples of Christ), USA, I.114-120; Methodist Church in Ireland, II.230ff.

[11] The aspect of enriching and vitalizing liturgical forms is especially underlined, cf., for example, the Presbyterian Churches in the USA, III.193,195-196, and in Canada, II.153; United Methodist Church, Central and Southern Europe, II.202; Evangelical Church in Baden, V.47,59; United Church of Canada, II.278.

catechetical instruction and our theological training of future pastors..." (III.146). The Church of Scotland regards BEM as an instrument of education and reflection (I.89) and the Evangelical Church of Westphalia testifies how discussions on BEM "led people to form groups in which 'learning in community' took place, causing a change of consciousness. We learn that congregations and church members must surrender their provincial self-satisfaction, overcome their own limitations and become open to ecumenical thought" (IV.151). The United Church of Christ, USA, adds to the implication of BEM for worship and education the suggestion that this document "calls us to hold in closer relationship our ministry of nurture and our ministry of prophetic servanthood in the cause of peace with justice throughout the world. It raises with new poignancy the essential place of spiritual formation of an order that will sufficiently equip us for faithfulness in the struggle with all unfaith that assaults the reign of God in human history" (II.334-335).

16. Implications of BEM for the renewal of the meaning, place and practice of *baptism* are considered by a large number of responses. The Uniting Church in Australia lists a number of challenges which reappear in many other responses: "In particular, we find ourselves challenged to be more vigilant against the practice of indiscriminate baptism, against the willingness of some to comply with a request for re-baptism, and against any confusion of baptism with naming ceremonies (B.16); to pay more serious attention to the nurture in faith of those baptized (B.12 and comm.); to consider how the celebration might be concentrated at particular festivals, viz., Easter, Pentecost and Epiphany, as in the early church (B.17); and to devise more opportunities for the baptized to reaffirm their faith, at the eucharist, at Easter and at the baptism of others (B.14 and comm.)" (V.157). The Federation of Evangelical Churches in the GDR adds work with parents and godparents to these points. It also acknowledges the danger of indiscriminate baptism, but considers that "in our environment, however, responsibility for the practice of baptism also includes the missionary endeavour to encourage people to be baptized and to believe". The ethical implications of baptism require that the baptized are helped to lead a life of witness and service (V.127).

17. The Evangelical Lutheran Church of Finland offers this list of challenges coming from BEM: the fundamental significance of baptism for Christian life and ecclesial practice, the administration of baptism in public worship services and at the great church festivals, a greater attention to the "symbolic meaning of the baptismal water", the close

connection between baptism and confirmation, the emphasis on "baptism being a lifelong process of growth into Christ", the communal nature of baptism and education in relation to baptism (III.117-118). These points occur in other responses as well, in different combinations and in varying detail, whereby the need to relate baptism and Christian education is especially stressed, also by Orthodox responses,[12] together with increased attention given to the whole process of Christian initiation including the proper understanding and place of confirmation and the question of admission of baptized children to holy communion.

18. The implications of the BEM section on the *eucharist* are taken up in the responses on an even broader scale which comprises eucharistic practice, liturgy and theology. Several quotations and references must again suffice to indicate points and concerns of many responses. The Evangelical Reformed Church of North West Germany states that the "comprehensive expositions on the institution and meaning of the eucharist are a helpful motivation for us to recognize and overcome a certain narrowness of our teaching and church life". This is exemplified by referring to "the joy of the Lord's supper" and the significance of the eucharist for the whole person and for all aspects of life, which can "liberate us from an exaggeratedly individualistic interpretation" (IV.95). Another church of the Reformed tradition, the Presbyterian Church in Wales, points to the well-known practice "to regard the Lord's supper as a brief appendage to a morning or evening preaching service. The essential unity of word and sacrament within the eucharist and the outline of the elements of the eucharistic liturgy... challenge us to consider whether our free and unstructured communion services are not in danger of omitting elements which results in an impoverishment of both the theological and liturgical significance of the rite". It also recognizes the "need for the centrality of praise and thanksgiving within the eucharist" and accepts the challenge to re-examine the way of dealing with the elements after the celebration by this comparison: "Reformed Christians would be horrified if pages of a discarded pulpit Bible were used to wrap up fish and chips! And yet we are often totally indifferent to the way in which the eucharist elements are disposed of" (II.170-171).

19. The Methodist Church of Southern Africa underlines the reminder "that the eucharist is a complete act of worship and not an isolated ritual tagged on at the end of a preaching service", that the eucharist "embraces all aspects of life" (E.20) which "should counter a pietistic approach to

---

[12] Cf. Russian, Bulgarian and Finnish Orthodox churches, II.7,13-14,26.

the sacrament", that it is a "foretaste of the kingdom and an expression of hope", and the response reflects on the communion for the sick "as a continuation of the church's liturgy" (II.239-240). The Evangelical Church of the Palatinate (mimeographed document) affirms that the aspects of thanksgiving and joy over God's new creation should find clearer expression in its worship. The Evangelical Church in Baden expresses the same intention and refers also to the Trinitarian dimension of the eucharist (V.43f.). "We acknowledge", state the American Baptist Churches in the USA, "that BEM offers us the opportunity to deepen our understanding of this 'memorial', to escape from a very 'thin' notion of 'remembrance', and to appreciate anew the way in which this commemoration draws us into deeper communion with God and is the occasion for Christ to be truly present" (III.260). Together with the dimension of praise and joy and the relation of the Lord's supper to creation and world, the United Protestant Church of Belgium mentions "the aspect of 'communio' with the Lord and among the faithful (E.19,20,21,24) as a corrective to a somewhat individualistic way of understanding the encounter with God". And it concludes: "Holy communion is not an optional extra to the preaching of the word any more than preaching is optional in a very elaborate eucharist celebration" (III.173).

20. Also the more "liturgically oriented" churches are ready to accept the challenge to broaden their understanding of the eucharist and to come to a more adequate correspondence between teaching and practice. The Orthodox Church of America states: "Although in most of our churches we have begun to participate more frequently and regularly in eucharistic communion and to understand and experience the church herself more fully as a eucharistic community, we still have not always realized the implications of the eucharist for church organization and administrative structures, for mission and ethical behaviour" (III.19). The Bulgarian and Russian Orthodox churches emphasize the "more frequent receiving of the communion, as had been the custom in the early church" (II.14,7,11). Lutheran responses affirm that their efforts at renewal of eucharistic theology, liturgy and practice in recent decades receive further impulses and insights from BEM, especially concerning the regaining of the eucharist as the central place for personal and communal faith and witness, the development of a broader, comprehensive Trinitarian understanding of the Lord's supper in terms of praise and thanksgiving, the cosmic dimension, the ethical implications, the elements of reconciliation and *communio*, the significance of *anamnesis* and *epiklesis*, and the

concerns of more frequent celebration and receiving of the eucharist, respect for the elements, distribution to the sick and admission of baptized children to the table of the Lord.[13] This, in fact, sums up most of what the churches have said about the eucharist in response to the third question.

21. The explicit or implicit responses to the third question which draw conclusions from the *ministry* section of the Lima document focus on questions of structure and actual practice in the respective churches. Aspects of the theology of ministry which occupy much space in the comments on the ministry section, are invoked only occasionally. Most responses indicate that in the churches many questions concerning the ordained ministry, other ministries, and the calling of the whole people of God are under discussion, that they are in need of clarification and more adequate implementation and that BEM is welcomed as a help in this self-critical and constructive assessment.

22. Reformation churches which have traditionally emphasized the priesthood of all baptized believers see a major challenge in a more concrete realization of their position. "In reality we have — in spite of sound biblical and reformational insights and the evoking of the Barmen theological declaration — a pastor's church where the church people are not only guided spiritually by their ministers, but very often intellectually patronized by the ordained incumbents of their parish," says the Evangelical-Reformed Church of North-West Germany (IV.97).[14] But also churches from other traditions use the opening paragraphs of the ministry section of BEM to ask how the calling and manifold gifts of the whole people of God can be more fully encouraged, respected and exercised in relation with and complementary to the special ministries of the church.[15]

23. A self-critical stance is also taken by churches which have preserved the threefold pattern of ministry, strongly supported by BEM. They willingly accept BEM's plea for a reform and better implementation of this structure: "However, the Episcopal Church [in the USA] has not yet asked how the potential of the threefold pattern of ministry can be

---

[13] Cf. Evangelical Church of the Augsburg Confession, Romania, IV.86; Church of Sweden, II.133-134; Lutheran Church of America, I.36-37; Evangelical-Lutheran Church of Denmark, III.112; North Elbian Evangelical Lutheran Church, I.47; Evangelical Lutheran Church in Brunswick, VI.47, and other examples.

[14] Cf. e.g., Church of Sweden, II.139; Evangelical Church of Hesse-Nassau, IV.135-136; Swiss Protestant Church Federation, VI.85-86; Presbyterian Church, USA, III.202.

[15] Cf. Methodist Church, GB, II.215; Anglican Church of Canada, II.44.

fully developed for the most effective witness for the Church in the world
— in its life, mission, ministry, canons, and the like" (II.61). In a similar
vein the Orthodox Church in America says: "Possessing the threefold
ministry, we are faced with the task of elucidating its meaning for the life
of the church today. We are grateful to the theologians of the Faith and
Order Commission for calling attention to this task. For we must admit
that our forms of ordained ministry have not always served effectively to
proclaim and manifest Christ's victory over the divisions of this broken
and fallen world" (III.23). Churches from other traditions declare their
openness to the threefold pattern of ministry. The European Continental
Province of the Moravian Church "expressly welcomes this (structure) as
it corresponds to its own history and also opens doors towards other
churches" (VI.121). "The threefold pattern of the church's ministry
should be studied afresh in our church," responds the Evangelical
Lutheran Church of Finland. "According to our confessions the ministry
is one, but they know and can accept the threefold pattern of the ministry
as a human institution" (III.123). This readiness for further study is
shared by several churches in the perspective of a proper diversity of
ministries.[16]

24. One element of the threefold pattern is the ministry of deacons.
Many responses refer to this issue. "Does not our church also need a
separate ministry of the diaconate, as part of the overall commission of
the church, to bear witness to the serving ministry of the church?" asks
the Evangelical Church in Baden (V.53). The Finnish Orthodox Church
says: "It is good that the BEM document also reminds the Orthodox of the
original nature of the ministry of a deacon. Nowadays there are many
possibilities and needs to develop the ministry of service in our church,
too" (II.28). Many plead for a reform of the diaconate, a clearer definition
of its role and relation to other ministries and a review of the issue of
ordination to the diaconate.[17] Another element of the threefold pattern,
the episcopate, is regarded by some responses as acceptable for the sake

---

[16] Cf. among others Evangelical Church of the Augsburg Confession, Romania, IV.90;
Evangelical Lutheran Church in Württemberg, V.29; Evangelical Church in Baden, V.52-
53; Methodist Church of Southern Africa, II.241; Presbyterian Church of Wales, II.173-
174; Evangelical Methodist Church, FRG, IV.180.

[17] E.g., Church of England, 77; United Methodist Church, USA, II.196; Methodist Church
in Southern Africa, II.242; Mission Covenant Church of Sweden, II.322; Anglican
Church of Canada, II.44; North Elbian Evangelical Lutheran Church, I.51; Evangelical
Church of Berlin-Brandenburg (Berlin West), VI.66; Evangelical Church of Kurhessen-
Waldeck, V.97.

of unity and the exercise of episkope,[18] while "episcopal" churches ask for a more appropriate implementation of this office in accordance with its theological basis and modern needs.[19] Several Reformation and Free churches express their readiness to consider the issue of apostolic succession in an open way.[20]

25. "Guiding principles" for the personal, collegial and communal forms of exercising the ministry (M.26 and 27) are welcomed and related to the existing situation in the churches.[21] "Many in the Church of Scotland find that discharge of the personal dimension at congregational level alone is inadequate: the life of the church is impoverished by the lack of a *pastor pastorum*; the mission of the church is debilitated by lack of the drive, initiative, and vision that one person in permanent official position can impart" (I.92). The comment of the Evangelical Lutheran Church of Iceland arises from a different tradition: "The guiding principles for the exercise of the ordained ministry in the church are a necessary admonition for us, where emphasis on the 'personal dimension' takes precedence over other emphases" (IV.71). Another aspect which is taken up as a challenge are the "conditions for ordination" (M.45-50),[22] and a few responses refer also to revision of ordination liturgies, the service of the ordained ministry to the unity and continuity of the church and a more appropriate understanding and exercise of authority.

4. Responses to the fourth question

26. In the *fourth question* from the preface of the Lima document the churches were asked to make suggestions *"for the ongoing work of Faith and Order as it relates to material of its text on 'Baptism, Eucharist and Ministry' to its long-range research project 'Towards the Common Expression of the Apostolic Faith Today'"*. In most cases the responses to this question are rather short and generally not limited to the apostolic

---

[18] Methodist Church of Southern Africa, II.242; Methodist Church, GB, II.215; Presbyterian Church of Wales, II.173-174.
[19] Orthodox Church of America, II.23; Church of England, III.77.
[20] Cf. e.g., Evangelical Church of Berlin-Brandenburg (Berlin West), VI.67; Federation of Evangelical Churches in the GDR, V.143; Methodist Church, GB, II.215; Methodist Church of Southern Africa, II.242-243.
[21] Federation of Evangelical Churches in the GDR, V.142; Church of England, III.77; Methodist Church, GB, II.215; Swiss Protestant Church Federation, VI.85-86.
[22] Evangelical Church of the Augsburg Confession, Romania, IV.92; Evangelical Lutheran Church in Württemberg, V.29; Russian and Bulgarian Orthodox Churches, II.11 and 14; United Methodist Church, USA, II.196-197.

faith project only. The comments on the three sections of BEM also contain, of course, numerous suggestions for further work on specific points.

27. The summary of the broader range of suggestions must start with the *follow-up of BEM*. Together with the many suggestions for continuing study and use of BEM goes the request to the Faith and Order Commission to document and evaluate the responses and to suggest directions for further work where major differences still remain. It is essential for this work "that the aim of mutual recognition and the continually increasing communion of the churches should not be lost sight of" (Evangelical Church of the Rhineland, V.92). This is closely connected with considerations, already described in part A of this chapter (paras 35-37), about the nature and forms of the *unity we seek* and the request for further study of this issue, especially with regard to what is essential for unity and what constitutes legitimate diversity. The perspective of such work is given, according to the Church of England, by the reminder of BEM "that unity and mission belong together. The unity of the church is not an end in itself but for the service of God and for mission to the world" (III.65).

28. A number of responses to the fourth question refer to topics for further work in relation to the three sections of BEM. On *baptism* the suggestion of the Baptist Union of Great Britain and Ireland "that any further work on baptism could be usefully done only in the wider context of Christian initiation" (I.74) reappears also in other responses, especially in the reference to baptism and confirmation.[23] The (Anglican) Church of Ceylon suggests to the Faith and Order Commission that "the mainline churches too must be made to think of baptism more in terms of an act of commitment and not merely in terms of a rite of initiation. Such an understanding would help to forward the mission of the church that has to proclaim the gospel among a plurality of religions" (IV.15). It is especially in relation to the *eucharist* section of BEM that several churches request further work on the relationship between word and sacrament.[24] The Church of Ceylon concludes from BEM that "the churches should actively pursue the need for a limited eucharistic sharing" and requests the Faith and Order Commission to promote such thinking among all the churches and groups, and help to

---

[23] Cf. e.g., Reformed Church in America, II.141; Presbyterian Church of Wales, II.168.
[24] Cf. e.g., Lutheran and Reformed Churches in France, III.143,147,164; Evangelical Church of Hesse-Nassau, IV.134; Waldensian and Methodist Churches in Italy, II.247.

make "this sacrament a sacrament of unity" (IV.16). Three topics for further work on the issue of the *ministry* of the church stand out in the responses: the ordination of women, the diaconate, and apostolic succession. The wider dimension of continuing work on the ministry is emphasized by the United Methodist Church, USA: "In considering the history of the church since apostolic times, we stress again the primacy of the mission of the gospel and the varieties of service it requires of ministers... Our last word about ministry, then, is the one by which God in Christ initiated it: mission" (II.197).

29. Many responses refer, of course, to the ongoing Faith and Order project "Towards the Common Expression of the Apostolic Faith Today" underlined in the fourth question. They affirm the significance of this project, relate suggestions on other topics to this study, remind Faith and Order, for example, to give proper consideration to the Old Testament, to include theologians from all parts of the world in this study, to make it a *contemporary* expression of the apostolic faith ("We all live under the threat of disaster. Some of us fear the apocalpyse tomorrow, others experience the apocalypse now. 'The Apostolic Faith *Today*' must speak to this situation")[25] and not to forget that "confession of faith is inadequately understood if it is thought of merely as assent to statements of belief. Properly understood, the Church's confession of faith is an act of obedience and an expression of praise addressed to God in response to his deeds of mercy and love".[26]

30. Many responses suggest two additional themes for the future work of Faith and Order which emerge directly from the Lima document and the responses to it: a reconsideration of the relationship between *scripture and Tradition* as an ecumenical investigation of the norms for Christian faith, life and unity, and a more comprehensive and focused study on *the church*. Such work on ecclesiology in an ecumenical setting is regarded by many as necessary because, according to the Roman Catholic Church, the goal of unity cannot be reached "without agreement on the nature of the church" (VI.40). The same conviction is expressed by the Church of England: "Only an explicit common understanding of the nature of the Church and its role as a credible and effective sign, instrument and sacrament of salvation will provide a secure foundation for the reconciliation of churches" (III.65). Accordingly, the Evangelical Church of Baden suggests: "In the continuation of what has been begun an attempt should

---

[25] Methodist Church, GB, II.217.
[26] Church of England, III.64.

be made to prepare a convergence text on the 'church'" (V.49). Other suggested themes also impose themselves either from the responses to BEM like *sacrament and sacramentality* or are brought to the attention of Faith and Order because they are not, or not sufficiently, dealt with in BEM: the *missionary dimension* of the church and its unity, *authority in the church* in terms of teaching authority and structures of decision-making, and the primacy of the *bishop of Rome*.

5. Conclusion

31. This summary of responses to the second, third and fourth questions from the preface to the Lima document is an indication, though a very limited one, of the remarkable degree to which churches have accepted the challenges implied in BEM and especially in the invitation to prepare an official response to this text. These challenges have led to critical self-examination and serious reflection on ways in which the already existing ecumenical community between the churches can be deepened on the way to visible unity and how the thinking and life of the churches can be renewed and enriched within and through this community. Only through such renewal can the churches properly respond not only to BEM, but also and in the first place to their common calling to unity and mission today. "Unless the work of Christ bears fruit in the reconciliation of Christians at the institutional as well as personal level, the church cannot function as an effective and credible witness to the gospel of reconciliation in a divided world" (Church of England, III.65).

Part Two

Clarifications and Major Issues for Further Work: Drafts

IV. Draft Clarifications and Comments on Critical Points

Introduction

Among the many comments, suggestions and critical remarks in the official responses of the churches to BEM quite a number refer to the same specific points in BEM or to more general points concerning the language and theological orientation of the document. In most of these cases a clarification seems to be possible which could remove misunderstandings caused by the text and open up the way to better mutual understanding on these points. Accordingly, the clarifications and comments which follow are a first attempt to reflect on the points raised in the responses. This will be done by way of interpretation of the BEM text and its theological intentions and by indicating insights gained from the responses and from further dialogue. It is hoped that this attempt may assist in developing the convergences expressed in BEM and facilitate their acceptance.

A. CLARIFICATIONS AND COMMENTS ON THE BAPTISM TEXT

1. The Holy Spirit before, in and after baptism (B.5)

Some responses questioned the first sentence in B.5, "The Holy Spirit is at work in the lives of people before, in and after their baptism", as though it implied a general and undifferentiated statement about the Holy Spirit at work throughout humankind. While the Holy Spirit may be said to be active in a general way throughout creation and history, the intention of BEM was to emphasize that the Spirit is at work in a special way leading people to baptism, continues to work in the act of baptism and nourishes the life of faith after baptism (cf. also B.14).

2. God's gift and human response (B.8)

a) Many churches ask for clarification concerning the statement of B.8 that "baptism is both God's gift and our human response to that gift".

b) The meaning was unfolded in the following sentence that "the necessity of faith for the reception of the salvation embodied and set forth in baptism is acknowledged by all churches". And then again at the end of B.10: "Within a fellowship of witness and service, Christians discover the full significance of the one baptism as the gift of God to all God's people. Likewise, they acknowledge that baptism, as a baptism into Christ's death, has ethical implications which not only call for personal sanctification, but also motivate Christians to strive for the realization of the will of God in all realms of life (Rom. 6:9ff.; Gal. 3:27-28; 1 Pet. 2:21-4:6)."

c) The responses to BEM themselves make clear that all the churches affirm God's initiative in the gift of salvation. Baptism expresses the priority of God's gracious initiative; and when the baptized profess their faith, they are professing what they have received, whether that profession be made directly at baptism or only later in life. Churches of every tradition also welcome the idea that baptism entails "life-long growth into Christ" (B.9), that baptized believers should "grow in the Christian life of faith" (B.10).

3. Terminology "infant baptism/believers' baptism" (B.11-12)

a) Several churches have expressed uneasiness and disagreement with regard to the terminology "believers' baptism" over against "infant baptism", because it seems to imply the suggestion that infants and children could not be called "believers" *(fideles)*. In some languages the term "baptism of adults" is indeed more common. The Commission, facing this problem already after comments on the Accra text (1974), decided to keep the usual English language terminology, used by Baptist churches and Disciples themselves and meanwhile common in ecumenical dialogue.[1]

b) In the text and in the commentary it is explained that the terminology does not prejudge the theological problems implied. Believers' baptism is circumscribed in B.11 as "baptism upon personal profession of faith" and as "baptism of believers who are able to make a personal confession of faith" and in B.12, "those baptized upon their own confession of faith".

---

[1] See Amsterdam 1948 para. 15; New Delhi 1961 para. 36; Montreal 1963 para. 111; *One Lord, One Baptism*, p.63; Accra 1974 paras 12-14; Louisville Consultation 1979, *passim* with some exceptions.

Such persons are not necessarily "adults" in a legal sense, but could also be children of a certain age after due preparation.

4. Equivalent alternatives (B.12 comm.)

Some churches ask what is meant by "equivalent alternatives" in the commentary to B.12. It is not the act of "infant baptism" and the act of "believers'/adult baptism" *in themselves* that are there proposed as "equivalent alternatives", but rather two total processes of initiation which the text recognizes.

5. Admission of baptized children to the eucharist (B.14 comm. (b))

a) According to many churches the relation of baptism and the eucharist, both sacraments of the new covenant, rooted in Jesus' ministry, is so intrinsic, that baptized children should be admitted to eucharistic communion. Due instruction of children in the meaning of the eucharist is regarded as a pedagogical and catechetical necessity. Several churches would welcome the opportunity for mutual consultation on this point.

b) The relation between baptism and eucharist, and the participation of the baptized in the whole liturgy of the church were more strongly expressed in the Accra text (see Accra B.1 and 6). Some churches with good reason wish to restore this emphasis. Three reasons in particular are mentioned in the responses.

  i) baptism has definite ecclesiological implications and is a basic bond and expression of the given unity in Christ (B.6) of which the mutual recognition of baptism is an important manifestation on the way towards "visible unity in one faith and one eucharistic communion" (By-laws of Faith and Order).

  ii) There is theological content common to both baptism and the eucharist, such as the theology of the covenant, participation in the death and resurrection of Christ, their pneumatological aspects and remission of sins. These could have been more clearly underlined in the text along with incorporation into the body of Christ in the commentary 14 (b).

  iii) In some traditions baptism and eucharist are always closely related in one service of initiation. The Orthodox churches admit infants, children or adults to the eucharist directly after baptism and chrismation; in the Roman Catholic and some other traditions when children and adults are baptized, they are confirmed and admitted to the eucharist in the same celebration, after due preparation as catechumens; in several churches coming from the Reformation a practice is developing of admitting baptized children to the eucharist after some catechetical preparation, whereas confirmation may come at a later age.

c) Churches baptizing children might further consider whether their participation in the eucharistic liturgy of the church with proper preparation and in the context of Christian nurture (see B.12) will contribute to theological convergence on the unity of the sacraments of membership in the body of Christ. As regards the structure of Christian nurture, those churches which practise infant baptism and those which only baptize children or adults upon a personal confession of faith, have much in common. All of them have to find ways towards responsible participation of children in the full congregational and liturgical life of the church (cf. B.12).

6. Terminology of "sign"

a) In the responses of the churches, the use of the term "sign" in the baptism section of BEM is often criticized as being either inadequate or ambiguous. Part of the difficulty resides in the fact that, in various languages and semiotic theories, terms like "sign" or "symbol" are heard and used in different ways, sometimes with a stronger meaning, sometimes with a weaker, sometimes in opposition to each other. Also in BEM itself, terms have different meanings and degrees of meaning in different contexts (compare, for example, the uses of "sign" and "signify": in B.2 "sign of new life", in B.6 "sign and seal of our common discipleship", in B.7 "sign of the Kingdom of God", in B.14 "sign of the gift of the Spirit", in B.15 "important sign and means", in B.19 "sign of the laying on of 'hands'", in B.21 "sign of the Kingdom").

b) When used in direct relation to baptism and God's work in it, it should be made clear that "sign" does not simply point towards, but actually participates in, the reality which it effectively conveys. Therefore, the term "sign" should be understood in the emphatic sense of "effective sign". This is what is meant by the term "sacrament" in most traditions. Cf. also "Clarifications", B.3, on the same question in the eucharist section, and "Major Issues", B. Sacrament and Sacramentality.

7. The principal agent in baptism

a) Responses have criticized formulations in BEM like "baptism is...", "baptism means...", "baptism makes...", "baptism initiates...", because they could suggest either a "mechanical" or "magical" efficacy in the sacramental rite as such or that the sacraments would be the work of the church independently of God's gracious activity. Such formulations were made for brevity's sake and are to be understood in the light of the initial statement that "baptism is a gift of God" (B.1). They have at their basis the common conviction that the Triune God is the principal agent in baptism. When the risen Lord commanded his followers to teach and to baptize in the name of the Father, the Son and the Holy Spirit, he assured them that he would accompany them to the end of the world (Matt. 28:18-20). The impression mentioned above could have been avoided, if the BEM text would occasionally have used formulations like "God through baptism..." or "in baptism, God through Christ in the Holy Spirit..."

b) There is agreement that the church is neither master over baptism or any other sacrament nor do the sacraments have their role and efficacy in themselves, independently of God's action through them.

8. Sin and forgiveness in baptism

a) Baptism according to BEM is for the forgiveness of sins (B.2-4). Several responses to BEM emphasize that this affirmation should have been made more strongly in the document, e.g., with regard to the institution of baptism (B.1, cf. Acts 2:38) and the description of its essential liturgical elements (B.20), where it is not mentioned. In the chapter on the "meaning of baptism" the theme might have been included and strengthened, e.g., in the following way.

b) Where BEM asserts that death and resurrection in Christ through baptism is the God-given act whereby "the power of sin is broken" (B.3), it could also have been acknowledged that in fact sin does occur again in Christian life after baptism so that Christians are called to struggle against it by God's grace throughout their entire lives. So it is that baptism begins a process of repentance and conversion in which forgiveness of sins is offered to believers by the God in whose name they are baptized.

9. Original sin

a) Some churches ask why the text on baptism did not use the term "original sin". This term has proved open to misunderstanding, but the reality envisaged by it was addressed in B.3 where it is said that by baptism "the old Adam is crucified with Christ... and the power of sin is broken". The same reality is also recognized in the commentary to B.12 where it is said that "the infant is born into a broken world and shares in its brokenness". Although they are without personal guilt, infants share with all people in the common human sinfulness.

b) This common human sinfulness, as well as the actual sins of individuals, is comprehended when it is said that "those baptized are pardoned, cleansed and sanctified by Christ" (B.4).

10. The relation between baptism and confirmation (B.14)

a) The responses to BEM reveal remarkable agreement on the conviction that God gives the Holy Spirit to those who die and rise with Christ in baptism. They show lack of agreement about how the anointing and sealing of the Spirit is to be expressed in the baptismal rite, and how it relates to confirmation and participation in the eucharist.

b) The churches, in fact, demonstrate changing attitudes and actions concerning confirmation in accordance with an increasing awareness that originally there was one complex rite of Christian initiation. Confirmation is still seen to be serving two different purposes. Some churches see confirmation as the special sign of the gift of the Spirit in the total process of initiation, others take confirmation above all as the occasion for a personal profession of faith by those baptized at an earlier age. All are agreed that the first sign in the process of initiation into the body of Christ is the rite of water baptism; all are agreed that the goal of initiation is nourishment in the eucharist. Whichever emphasis is made in the understanding of confirmation, each is related to baptism and holy communion. This might be taken as a hopeful sign that the churches are coming to an understanding of initiation as a unitary and comprehensive process, even if its different elements are spread over a period of time. The total process vividly embodies the coherence of God's gracious initiative in eliciting our faith.

B. CLARIFICATIONS AND COMMENTS ON THE EUCHARIST TEXT

1. The term "eucharist"

a) While all churches recognize the appropriateness of returning thanks *(eucharistia)* to God for the gift of salvation, some responses consider that the dominant use of the name "eucharist" in BEM overemphasizes the movement from the church to God. Protestant churches ask for greater use of the names "Lord's supper" or "holy communion" which are more familiar to them and which express, they feel, the prior importance of the divine gift; the nature of these terms also allows and requires distinct mention to be made of the preaching or proclamation which is central to the liturgy of the word. According to BEM, however, the notion of "eucharist" is primarily rooted in the thanksgiving of Jesus himself to the Father, which is then commemorated in the eucharistic liturgy of the church. Granted that the eucharist, in the broader sense, has several "aspects" (E.2), it would have been wise — and it remains appropriate — to make fuller use of the variety of scriptural and traditional names in order to suggest the richness of its meaning.

b) The Lima text uses the term "eucharist" in several ways, which has led to some misunderstanding. Basically, it means the entire service, "one complete act" (E.2), "a single whole" (E.27), "which always includes both word and sacrament" (E.3). Often the stress falls on the sacramental part of the service, the "sacramental meal" (E.1,31) or "eucharistic meal" (E.2,12,13,14), where the word of prayer, the "great thanksgiving" *(eucharistia,* E.3), the "sacrifice of praise" *(anaphora,* E.4), leads to the "eucharistic communion" (E.2,19).

2. Eucharist as the central act of worship (cf. E.1, last sentence)

a) When it is said that the eucharist "continues as the central act of the Church's worship" (E.1), this statement is made in relation to the central place of the eucharistic celebration in the life of the church from the time of the apostles and the reference is to the full worship service, "which always includes both word and sacrament" (E.3). Both by its meaning and function the service of word and sacrament occupies a central place in the life of the church. Both "the preached word" and "the eucharistic meal" are seen as having "the *anamnesis* of Christ" as their "very content"; therefore "each reinforces the other" (E.12). The reference to "central act" also implies that the eucharist should not be overshadowed by other liturgical services, and it certainly does not imply that the eucharist is the only liturgical occasion where the saving event of Jesus Christ is presented to the community.

b) In terms of liturgical structures, it may be appropriate to envisage the single service of word and sacrament as an ellipse with two foci. All churches recognize that a service of the word may have its own integrity. The question then remains of the appropriate frequency of the eucharistic celebration in the narrower sense, i.e., the Lord's supper or holy communion (E.30). The responses of many Protestant churches declare — sometimes with acknowledgment of the stimulus provided by the Lima text — their acceptance in principle of a weekly, or Sunday, eucharist. The Orthodox and Roman Catholic churches, long familiar with the eucharist as the principal service of Sunday, now experience a renewal of preaching.

c) When BEM speaks of word in the fullest sense, it means the word of God by which the world was made, who became incarnate in Jesus Christ, and who now comes among us through the living voice of the gospel in preaching, in sacraments and in service. In Christian worship the words of scripture and of the church's proclamation, confession and prayers all serve the saving presence and action of the word himself. The responses to BEM remind us that the sacraments have often been understood as "visible words".

3. Terminology in relation to the eucharist

a) Many responses have criticized the oscillating use of the term "sign" in many and diverse contexts in the section on the eucharist (E.1,4,5,15,21,22,24,29). The matter is complicated by the fact that some responses also introduce their own interpretations of "sign" and "symbol" (the term "symbol" is used only once, in E.1 "symbolic words and actions").

b) In most instances the immediate context in which "sign" is used interprets its meaning, e.g., the more general use of "sign" in phrases like "sign of peace" in E.21 or "signs of renewal" in E.22, while in phrases like "the living and effective sign of his [Christ's] sacrifice" in E.5 or "bread and wine become the sacramental signs of Christ's body and blood" in E.15, "sign" should be understood as not simply pointing towards, but actually participating in, the reality which it effectively conveys. Nevertheless, it should be admitted that BEM should have been more precise and consistent in its terminology. Cf. also "Clarifications and Comments" A.6, on the same question in the baptism section, and also V. "Major Issues", B. Sacrament and Sacramentality.

4. *"Anamnesis"* and *"Epiklesis"*

a) In general the references in BEM to *anamnesis* and *epiklesis* have found wide approval. But several responses have insisted that *anamnesis* and *epiklesis* should be presented as closely belonging together. Concerning *anamnesis* further clarification of this concept is asked for in several responses. With *epiklesis*, questions are raised concerning the relation of the invocation of the Holy Spirit to Christ's word of promise and, connected with this, concerning the invocation of the Spirit on the elements and, thirdly, the role of the church on the "epicletic" character of the whole eucharistic action.

b) Here it is necessary to take account of the full Trinitarian context. *Anamnesis* (memorial) and *epiklesis* (invocation) belong together, since

Christ and the Spirit belong together in an "indissoluble union" (E.14 comm.). The crucified and risen Christ is the living and active content of the "memorial" in word and meal (E.5-6,12), and the Spirit is "invoked" as the immeasurable strength of love which makes the eucharistic event possible and continues to make it effective (E.14-17). Every good gift of the Father reaches us through the Son in the Holy Spirit. "The word comes to the element and so there is the sacrament," says St Augustine,[1] and "that which is brought by human hands to the point of being the visible species is not sanctified to be such a great sacrament except by the invisible working of the Spirit of God".[2]

Anamnesis

c) In the Old Testament, various objects and actions in worship serve "as a memorial *(zikkaron)* for the children of Israel before the Lord" (Ex. 28:12,29, 30:16, 39:7; Lev. 23:24; Num. 10:9f., 41:54). At the institution of the passover and unleavened bread, it is commanded that "this day shall be for you a memorial, and you shall keep it as a feast to the Lord" (Ex. 12:14), and that "it shall be to you as a sign on your hand and as a memorial between your eyes, that the law of the Lord may be in your mouth; for with a strong hand the Lord has brought you out of Egypt" (Ex. 13:9). Given by God, the memorial not only serves to remind the children of Israel of the past mercies of God as a ground for their present obedience; it also enables the people to recall before God his past promises and deeds with thanksgiving, and in prayer for new blessings.

d) In the New Testament, it is the incarnate Son of God who is the agent of God's saving work. On the eve of his redemptive sacrifice, Christ gave to his followers a "memorial": *Touto poieite eis ten emen anamnesin* (Luke 22:19; 1 Cor. 11:24,25). Because Christ has been raised from the dead and exalted to the right hand of the Father, he can be present to his followers who assemble in his name to do what he commanded for his remembrance until he comes again (1 Cor. 11:26). It is an effective proclamation of his death and a means for receiving its benefits, including access to God.

e) Thus the Lord's supper is neither the occasion of a simple mental recollection of Christ and his death, nor yet a repetition of Calvary. It is rather a means graciously given by Christ himself for the realization of his

---

[1] *Treatises on John's Gospel*, 80.3=PL 35, 1840.
[2] *On the Trinity*, III.4.10=PL 42, 874.

presence. In the Holy Spirit, Christ comes to us, clothed in his mighty acts, and gathers us into his self-offering to the Father, in whom is eternal life.

Epiklesis

f) The Holy Spirit "rested" on the incarnate Son (John 1:33). The exalted Christ in turn joins the Father in "sending" the Spirit (John 14:16f., 26, 15:26, 16:7). The Holy Spirit brings the things of Christ to remembrance (John 14:26), takes the things of Christ and announces them (John 16:14). That Christ is not thereby reduced to passivity is shown by the fact that he can be said to "come" to his followers (John 14:3,18,23). It is in the Holy Spirit that the Son has chosen to come to us with the blessings of the Father.

g) In invoking the Holy Spirit *(epiklesis)*, the church is therefore claiming the promises of Christ, with the Lord's own assurance that prayers in his name will be graciously heard (John 14:13f., 16:23f.). The invocation of the Holy Spirit is the church's grateful recognition that it remains utterly dependent on the grace of God. The church cannot compel the presence of Christ but only receive it in the Holy Spirit. In the Holy Spirit, the church has access through Christ to the Father (Eph. 2:18).

h) The question of an *epiklesis* both on the community and on the elements (cf. E.14 and comm., E.27) needs further clarification. Some churches have doubted or rejected such form of *epiklesis* that is "constitutive" or invokes the Holy Spirit upon the elements (cf. "Responses", C.3). The Lima text did not discuss the form of *epiklesis*. It mentioned only the invocation of the Spirit on both the elements and the community as a traditional part of many liturgies (E.27) since the time of the early church (E.14 comm.). Perhaps the following perspective can be helpful. The invocation of the Spirit on the elements should never be isolated from the *epiklesis* on the community, while an *epiklesis* on the community assembled for the Lord's supper implies a reference to bread and wine, which "become the sacramental signs of Christ's body and blood" (E.15). Such a perspective in no way diminishes the significance of Christ's own words of institution.

5. Real presence

a) The ecumenically important issue of Christ's presence in the Lord's supper seems to have found a widely accepted solution in BEM. But the responses indicate that some questions remain about an adequate interpretation of the mystery of Christ's presence, its mode and especially its relation to the elements of bread and wine. Also the expression that this presence is "unique" should be further clarified.

b) It would be quite contrary to the overwhelming tradition of Christianity, and to the scriptures as there interpreted, to hold that the bread and wine had no part in Christ's presence at the Lord's supper. On the other hand, no church holds that Christ's eucharistic presence is limited to the bread and wine: Christ is present in the assembly gathered for prayer in his name (Matt. 18:20; Col. 3:16), in the reading of the scriptures which bear testimony to him (John 20:31), in the proclamation of the gospel concerning him (Luke 10:16; Rom. 10:17), and in the hearts of believers (Gal. 2:20; Col. 1:27). It is within this universe of meaning that any ecumenical confession of Christ's presence in the eucharist must be made.

c) It is also generally believed that the presence of the crucified and risen Christ at the supper is a pneumatic presence, a presence by the power of the Holy Spirit. That is common ground. It may be agreed, too, that Christ's presence is a mystery, in the sense that it cannot happen except for the sheer grace of God.

d) According to the scriptural records, Christ's institution of the supper includes both a gift ("this is my body", "this is my blood of the covenant") and a command ("take, eat...", "drink from this, all of you", "do this in remembrance of me, *eis ten emen anamnesin*"). There is room and need, therefore, for human acceptance of the gift and human obedience to the command. The church assembled in obedience needs to hear the words of promise spoken by someone in the name of the Lord (the *verba testamenti*): and the whole action is utterly dependent on the Holy Spirit, whom the church therefore appropriately invokes *(epiklesis)*. Only then can the bread be eaten and the wine drunk for communion with Christ.

e) Some would be content to leave it there. But once the question of the elements has been raised, it will not go away. In so far as erroneous answers threaten the faith, the question must be faced. It would be important that the Orthodox churches explain to others what they mean by the transformation of the elements *(metabole)*; that the Roman Catholic Church explore with others how what is "most aptly called transubstantiation" (Council of Trent) may otherwise be expressed; that those Protestants who deny any "essential change" in the elements state what they are thereby affirming. Here the dialogue remains open after the Lima text.

6. Sacrifice

a) The sacrificial character of the eucharist, another issue of controversy, has been presented in BEM in a manner which is seen as a way to overcome past controversies. Several responses, however, ask for further clarification of notions like "offering" and "sacrifice" in relation to the soteriological meaning of the saving act of Christ's death.

b) Christ "offered himself to God through the eternal Spirit" (Heb. 9:14). Christ now "ever lives to make intercession for us" (Heb. 7:25). When Christ, in instituting the eucharist on the eve of his passion, commanded his followers to "do this in remembrance of me, *eis ten emen anamnesin*", he delivered the bread with the words "this is my body", and the cup with the words "this is my blood of the new covenant" (Matt. 26:28; Mark 14:24) or "this cup is the new covenant in my blood" (Luke 22:20; 1 Cor. 11:25).

c) All churches affirm that Christ's sacrifice is unique — sufficient, unrepeated, unsupplemented. All affirm that the church is, by the Spirit, graciously included in the access which Christ's sacrifice gives to the Father (Eph. 2:18). All agree that the benefits of Christ's saving work are gratefully received in and by communion, made possible by the Holy Spirit (cf. 2 Cor. 13:14). All agree that, in Christ, Christians are to present themselves, body and soul, as a living sacrifice to God, consecrated by the Holy Spirit (Rom. 12:1f.; 1 Cor. 6:11,19).

d) Different theological expressions and visions are used in various traditions in order to relate the order of sign and sacrament in the eucharist to the unique sacrifice of Christ.

7. Cross and forgiveness in the eucharist

a) Some churches have been unable to recognize in the eucharist section of the text their own convictions about the centrality of Christ's cross and the forgiveness of sins for the significance of the sacrament.

b) In setting forth an inclusive concept of *anamnesis* the text does not lose sight of the centrality of the cross: the risen Christ is also forever the crucified one (E.1,5,14). The love of God which the sacrament communicates is that "by which Jesus loved his own 'to the end'" (John 13:1 cited in E.1). The joy of the resurrection is never to be seen apart from the significance of Christ's sacrificial death — a fact which might have been highlighted more in E.24.

c) On the forgiveness of sins it is true that E.1 (on the institution of the eucharist) only refers to, but does not quote, the Matthean text of Jesus' words, in which the assurance of forgiveness is contained, even though this version is the preferred one of most liturgical texts. However, this meaning of the eucharist is clearly set forth in E.2, and in E.9 we find the affirmation that the eucharist enables us to pray through Christ "as justified sinners". The chapter on the celebration of the eucharist sees an act of repentance as a constituent part of the celebration (E.27), and in E.21 we find reference to mutual forgiveness within the Christian community expressed within the liturgy. All that is said about receiving forgiveness in the eucharist is to be understood in the light of what is said in the baptism section, at B.8 and B.12, on the necessity of faith and growth in faith for the reception of salvation.

8. Judgment in the eucharist

Some responses feel that the theme of judgment is too weak in the text. BEM could have stated more plainly St Paul's sombre warning that the sacrament, when received in an unworthy manner, may be received unto judgment (1 Cor. 11:29). Although the Pauline text is not cited this idea is present in what E.20 says about the social implications of the eucharist. This is, however, criticized in some responses as being too exclusively ethical and "horizontal" though such emphasis would find legitimation in some modern exegeses of 1 Corinthians 11:27-33. The relation between judgment and personal salvation should, therefore, have been included, e.g., in E.13, where it is said that faith is necessary for discerning the body and blood of Christ. In this connection BEM should also have been more explicit about adequate moral and spiritual preparation for sharing in communion.

9. Law and gospel (E.20)

a) Most of the churches welcome the accent placed on the ethical implications of the eucharist (E.20,24). In some responses, however, it is indicated that the connection between the eucharistic celebration and the active participation in the "ongoing restoration of the world's situation and the human condition" (E.20) is not sufficiently clarified. The eucharistic challenge to get involved in social, economic and political life could suggest a gradual realization of the kingdom of God in this world or even be taken as a condition for receiving salvation in the eucharist. One of the Lutheran churches goes so far as to suggest that such activism represents an unacceptable mixture of law and gospel.

b) To this interpretation of the text it may be answered that participation in the ongoing restoration of human conditions and in the fight against all kinds of injustice is a consequence of the gospel received in the

Lord's supper. When E.20 says that "the eucharist embraces all aspects of life", and that eucharistic celebration "demands reconciliation and sharing" among all people, this presupposes E.2: "In accordance with Christ's promise, each baptized member of the body of Christ receives in the eucharist the assurance of the forgiveness of sins (Matt. 26:28) and the pledge of eternal life (John 6:51-58)". The relation of the eucharist to the mission of the Christians to the world is clearly stated in E.24: "Reconciled in the eucharist, the members of the body of Christ are called to be servants of reconciliation among men and women and witnesses of the joy of resurrection. As Jesus went out to publicans and sinners and had table-fellowship with them during his earthly ministry, so Christians are called in the eucharist to be in solidarity with the outcast and to become signs of the love of Christ who lived and sacrificed himself for all and now gives himself in the eucharist."

C. CLARIFICATIONS AND COMMENTS ON THE MINISTRY TEXT

1. Ordained ministry and the calling of the whole people of God (M.1-6)

a) Practically all responses to BEM have praised paragraphs M.1-6. Many regretted, however, that the rest of the ministry section does not sufficiently carry through this comprehensive concept of "the calling of the whole people of God" but concentrates on the ordained ministry.

b) One reason for this is the decision in the development of the BEM text to focus attention on the ecumenically controversial issues which are, of course, related specifically to the understanding and structures of the ordained ministry. Thus, this section was not intended to be a complete ecclesiological treatise on the ministry. Nevertheless, references to the inter-relation of the ordained ministry and the ministries, gifts and co-responsibility of the whole people can be found in paragraphs 7,8,12, comm. 13,15,16, comm. 16,17, comm. 17,21,23,26, comm. 26,27,31, comm. 31,32,33,40,41. The commentary to 13 (which according to some responses could have been part of the text), e.g., says: "Since the ordained ministry and the community are inextricably related, all members participate in fulfilling these functions."

c) However, in many places this inter-relation is mentioned only in passing, in asides. It should — and easily could — be more fully developed. Especially the diverse roles played by lay persons in the worship assembly of the church, the co-responsibility of the laity for leadership in the life of the church at all levels (presbyteries, synodical structures, commissions, etc.) and the involvement and participation of all the people of God in different forms of expressing the apostolic tradition and continuity of the church could have been expressed more directly and explicitly, e.g., in M.12,15,26,27 and in 34.

d) Such a broader perspective, which should however not obscure the specificity of the ordained ministry, might also contribute to a better understanding of the problems relating to ordained ministry itself as well as to common ecclesiological orientations which seem to be, according to many responses, the precondition for further convergence on the ordained ministry.

2. Ministry as constitutive (M.8)

a) The statement in M.8, that the ordained ministry "is constitutive for the life and witness of the Church", is considered by several responses as claiming something for the ministry which is due only to Christ and his word and sacrament.

b) Indeed, the ordained ministers are not the foundation of the church which is, according to the New Testament, Jesus Christ (1 Cor. 3:11) or the apostles and prophets (Eph. 2:20; Rev. 21:14); nor did the ordained ministers come first and lay people only later (cf. M.10: The Twelve "represent the whole people of God and at the same time exercise a special role in the midst of that community". And M.11: "Christ continues through the Holy Spirit to choose and call persons into the ordained ministry..."). It is Christ's continuing presence in word and sacrament, through the Holy Spirit, which is constitutive for the church. This implies, however, that for the sake of the ongoing life and mission of the church there must be persons, called by God, sent by Christ, assisted by the Holy Spirit and recognized by the people of God, to preach the word, to celebrate the sacraments, to bring together and guide the Christian community in faith, hope and love (cf. M.13). In terms of this service of Christ and of the community the ordained ministry is therefore constitutive or essential.

3. Focus of unity (M.8 and 14)

a) The formulation in M.8 that the ordained ministry is a "focus of its (i.e., the church's) unity" and in M.14 that this ministry "is the visible focus of the deep and all-embracing communion between Christ and the members of his body" has been criticized in responses. They would rather see Christ himself as the focus of unity in M.8 and the Lord's supper as the focus of communion between Christ and the members of his body in M.14.

b) Where the text speaks about the relation of the ministry to the unity of the Christian community it uses both the indefinite and the definite article: "*A* focus of unity" (M.8 and comm. 14) and "*the* focus of unity" (M.14 and comm. 13). In order to avoid the impression of an exclusive understanding of the phrase, the indefinite article should have been used in all instances. The communion and unity both within a church and between churches is indeed visibly manifested and maintained by a diversity of means.

c) However, where the multiplicity of gifts is fostered and employed in a Christian community there is also the need to hold these gifts together in order that they serve in common the life and witness of the church. Also the many local communities require a service of unity in order to express and preserve their communion within one church. Therefore there must be persons whose ministry includes in a continuous and representative manner the task of serving the unity within and among churches. Thus, among the various instruments of unity the ordained ministry carries its special responsibility to preserve and renew unity in the faith of the gospel. This seems to be a growing ecumenical agreement which could have been more fully and consistently developed in BEM.

4. Representation (M.14)

a) The idea of "representation", as formulated in the last sentence of M.14, and also used in M.11 and 8 and in the commentary to M.13, raised questions for many churches. Some have understood "to represent" or "in a representative way" in a merely functionalistic sense and would have preferred it to have clearly said that the presiding minister is "the icon of Christ" or that the minister acts *in persona Christi*. For other churches, mainly Reformation and Free churches, the latter understanding of "representation" would be rather alien. The task of "representing Christ" is the calling of all members of the community, they are inclined to say. For some, this would imply that the presidency of the eucharist could, therefore, under certain circumstances and conditions, be entrusted also to non-ordained members of the church.

b) Within this discussion on "representation", attention needs to be given to biblical perspectives on representation as when Christ says of those whom he appoints to preach and teach the word, "whoever hears you hears me" (Luke 10:16; cf. 2 Cor. 5:20). The ecumenical community should also hear the arguments coming from apostolic times to relate the presidency of the eucharist to the ordained leadership of the eucharistic community (cf. Heb. 13:7ff.; Ignatius, Smyrn. 8:1; cf. Trall 2:1; Magn. 6:1; Rom. 7:2). Not these persons in their own right, but precisely their public function (presidency) in the proclamation of the word and at the table of the Lord is an effective sign of the presence of Christ in the community. In this way they express the *koinonia* of all the baptized with the one body of Christ of all times and places, in which Christ himself is the one who presides in the eucharist. Accordingly the last sentence of M.15 is to be read in the light of E.29, so that the following understanding could emerge: it is the ordained minister who, in presiding at the Lord's supper, publicly represents the divine initiative and the *koinonia* with the church of all times and places.

5. Priesthood (M.17)

a) The commentary to M.17 has been favourably received by nearly all responses, whereas problems arise with the text of the paragraph itself. Some miss there a specific reference to the eucharistic sacrifice which is considered to be intrinsically related to the priestly character of the ordained ministry. Others, on the contrary, fear a confusion between the unique priesthood of Christ and the priestly service of the ordained ministry in its intercessory task. Such a confusion cannot in any way be seen in BEM.

b) Several point out that the reference to Romans 12:1 is inappropriate, because this text does not refer to the priestly character of the ordained ministry which is at stake here, whereas the reference to Romans 15:16 in the commentary would, indeed, refer to the apostolic ministry itself.

6. Ordination of women (M.18)

a) The responses of the churches to the section on the ministry of men and women in the church (M.18,54) show dissatisfaction with the inconclusiveness of BEM on this issue. While some churches express disappointment over BEM's failure to provide a forthright affirmation of the ordination of women, others register disapproval for what they see as BEM's implicit bias in this direction. Such criticisms reflect the fact that this issue is insufficiently developed in the document and also that there are serious differences between the churches on this point.

b) While revealing serious disagreements on the issue of the ordination of women, the responses to BEM show that the issue of the place and role of women in the church's various ministries and functions is receiving growing attention. There appears to be increasing willingness in all churches to include women in ministries previously exercised predominantly, if not exclusively by men, e.g. theological scholarship, teaching, missionary work, pastoral care and counselling, administration, etc. In churches having a diaconate, whether or not this office is considered to be "ordained", most churches are ready to include qualified women beside qualified men in this position. Such is even the case for some churches having the "threefold ministry" (viz. Orthodox and Anglican) and, as such, has significant implications for understanding ministry generally, and priesthood in particular, i.e., the relationship between bishops, presbyters and deacons, as well as the priesthood of all the believers.

c) Criticism in the churches' responses directed to the last part of section M.18, and its commentary (18) on the two views regarding the ordination of women is also well taken. The formulation of the two basic views on the issue is inadequate. Both those who oppose the ordination of women and those who support it ground their positions in an "understanding of the gospel" with "biblical and theological reasons". Those opposed do not simply refer to "the force of nineteen centuries of church tradition" which "must not be changed". The theological, Christological and anthropological convictions expressed in the respective arguments concerning the place and service of women in the church (though greatly developed since BEM's publication in 1982 through theological research and reflection, church meetings and reports, and ecumenical dialogue and consultation), still require deeper and fuller elaboration within the multilateral context provided by the Faith and Order Commission.

d) The responses testify to a new willingness to enter into a serious and open debate. Such a debate would need to clarify what are the central issues and to show the complexity of those issues and how they interrelate. Judgments have to be made, therefore, with reference to each of the following: God's self-relevation in creation, history and in the particularity of the incarnation; the authority of scripture, Tradition, reason and experience; the nature and purpose of the church, how the church comes to make a decision on matters of faith and order when churches remain divided and how decisions are received in life; the priesthood of ordained ministers in relation to the priesthood of Christ and the priesthood of the whole people of God; the nature of women and men created in the image of God; the evaluation of cultural differences and the priority of the church's mission. Hence the debate on the ordination of women is related to issues raised in other parts of this response, not least of all to the three major issues which demand further theological work, cf.

chapter V. Any further debate will need to take account of the experience of those churches which ordain women to a ministry of word and sacrament as well as of the reasons that cause others to hesitate or even to protest. The seriousness with which the churches have responded to the Lima text provides a new context of commitment for such an open debate.

e) Some of the responses suggest that the fact of the ordination or non-ordination of women is an obstacle to mutual recognition and reconciliation of ministries. Nevertheless no church claims that women's ordination precludes further efforts towards mutual recognition of ministries nor some growth in communion between the churches.

7. Threefold ministry (M.19-25)

a) Though most responses seem to have no fundamental problem with the question of a threefold ministry — as long as this is not conceived in a narrow or inflexible manner — many responses from Reformation and Free churches understood M.22 as making a particular historically developed pattern (cf. M.19) an indispensable condition of unity. This they cannot accept (cf. M.52 and 53).

b) In response to this interpretation it should be noted that M.51-55 did not make the possession or adoption of the threefold pattern a condition of recognition of ordained ministries (cf. esp. M.52). In addition, BEM fully recognized the need for reforms with regard to the threefold pattern. And, finally, the proposal to accept the threefold pattern for the sake of unity was not formulated in M.22 in terms of an indispensable condition, but rather as a means to this end.

c) Many responses seem to understand the Lima text on ministry, as though it aimed at the restoration of the threefold pattern of bishop, presbyter and deacon at the cost of the rich variety of other institutional forms of ministry in the church. In M.7(b) as well as in M.32-33 such other functions and institutional forms were positively mentioned. There is no fundamental disagreement among the churches as to the need and functions of these other forms of ministry being a God-given and appropriate expression of the multiform apostolic mission of the whole people of God.

d) Attention, however, should have been given in BEM to the ministerial functions of, e.g., elders in the Reformed/Presbyterian tradition, which express the participation of the community in the preaching of the word, the celebration of the sacraments and the leadership of the church (cf. M.27). The position of such ministers, however, with regard to the ordained ministry is unclear, as is evidenced in the responses, precisely in those churches which have introduced those functions at or after the Reformation. It is, therefore, necessary to further clarify their position. In such a study the specific problem of the existing forms of diaconate and of non-ordained deacons compared to the role of the ordained deacons, as proposed in M.22,24 and 31, should be dealt with.

e) A third issue here is raised by those churches which, appealing to a centuries-old tradition, prefer to speak of *one ordained ministry*, centred in the ministry of the local pastor. They accept, however, a certain differentiation in this one ministry and many of them would be prepared to adopt the threefold pattern for the sake of church unity provided that ordination to the episcopate does not imply a "higher degree" of ordination and that the function of ordained deacons be clarified.

f) Such a position is not totally alien to some churches which have kept the threefold pattern and where there is only one sacrament of ordination and one *ordo ministerii*, with diverse rites and functions. If these churches speak about the sacramental nature of all these rites of ordination, some of them distinguish between the *making* of deacons, the *ordaining* of priests and the *consecrating* of bishops. At the Second Vatican Council, the Roman Catholic Church drew on an Eastern patristic tradition in understanding episcopal ordination as the "fullness of the 'sacramentum ordinis'". Such "fullness" ("plenitude") in no way diminishes the "completeness" ("perfectio") of the ordination to the other ministries.

8. Episkope (M.21-23)

a) The question has been raised in responses concerning the exact theological foundation and structure of episkope as distinguished from episcopacy.

b) The ministry text distinguishes between *episkope* (M.21,23,53a) and episcopate (M.36 comm., 37,38). To exercise *episkope* is to have a function of pastoral leadership, oversight and co-ordination in the church. "In the first generation, apostles had exercised *episkope* in the wider church. Later Timothy and Titus are recorded as having fulfilled a function of *episkope* in a given area. Later again this apostolic task is carried out in a new way by the bishops" (M.21). A ministry of *episkope* is a gift of the Holy Spirit and "necessary to express and safeguard the unity of the body" (of Christ) (M.23). The text should perhaps have expressed more clearly that the function of *episkope* is exercised in various forms (M.53a) at all levels of the life of the church. According to circumstances it may be exercised in a personal, collegial or communal way.

c) Thus, the function of *episkope* is not limited to episcopacy, which is commonly understood as the system of church government by bishops, although many churches doubt whether an *episkope* without bishops would meet the full criteria of apostolic tradition.

9. Collegiality and synodality (M.27)

a) The issue of *collegiality* in M.27 has raised several questions in the responses, especially with regard to the second sentence of the paragraph: "At the level of the local eucharistic community there is need for an ordained minister acting within a collegial body." Does this mean a group of ordained ministers working together in a pastoral team, or could the college also include lay persons with special functions in the community? Either way would express the desired element of collegiality at all levels of church life because it enables consultation, co-operation and shared responsibility among the members of the college.

b) Nearly all churches have developed *synodal structures* such as parish councils and diocesan or regional or provincial synods, or wider and even universal bodies. This assures that "the exercise of the ordained ministry is rooted in the life of the community and... the community's effective participation in the discovery of God's will and the guidance of the Spirit" (M.26). Thus, all who are members of synodical bodies share in the decision-making processes of the church, the fresh interpretation of the gospel and the renewal of the life of the church. Such structures give concrete expression to the fundamental conciliarity of the church, its solidarity beyond the boundaries of the local congregation, and its worldwide identity, of which they are the voices.

c) Several responses request a dialogue on universal *primacy*. Such a future dialogue on the understanding and function of a primacy of one or some of the episcopal sees, should place the discussion within the framework of this same universal conciliarity which necessarily includes the issue of universal reception.

d) A number of responses also noted that BEM did not directly address the issue of *authority* in terms of structures of decision-making and authoritative teaching. In future work of the Faith and Order Commission on ecclesiology this issue will receive major attention.

10. Functions of the ministry (M.28-31)

a) The description of the functions of bishops, presbyters and deacons within the threefold ministry in M.29-31 was unsatisfactory according to many responses.

b) There are indeed so many cultural and time-bound differences of tasks and functions that a uniform description is hardly possible. One way would be to indicate only the specific functions, starting with the diaconate and then successively coming to the functions which are the special responsibility of presbyters and of bishops.

11. Episcopal succession (M.37-38)

a) Despite the fact that most responses have welcomed the distinction in BEM between apostolic tradition and episcopal succession as an important step forward, a considerable number of responses from Reformation and Free churches remain unpersuaded by the arguments in favour of episcopal succession as an important element in apostolic tradition, let alone a condition for the recognition of ministries as some churches would demand.

b) For many on both sides of the issue the question of episcopal succession remains the most difficult problem for further dialogue on ministry. Behind this issue lie significant ecclesiological questions. It can, therefore, only be tackled in the framework of a broader, more intensified discussion on ecclesiology in Faith and Order.

12. Sacramental understanding of ordination

a) In their responses to BEM, the Roman Catholic and the Orthodox churches asked that the sacramental nature of ordination be more clearly expressed. On the other hand, many Protestant churches insisted that ordination is not to be understood as a sacrament and accordingly not to be put on the same level as baptism and the Lord's supper.

b) The difference between the understanding of ordination as a "sacramental sign" (M.41-43) or a sacrament and the refusal to apply the term "sacrament" to ordination seems to have its source in different (e.g., broader or more narrow) concepts of sacrament and sacramentality which in turn have their origin in the controversies of the time of the Reformation and since that time. If this is recognized and further clarified (cf. V. "Major Issues", B. Sacrament and Sacramentality), it could be shown that the mutually contradictory positions in the responses may not be as far apart as first appears.

c) The responses agree that ordination is not just a purely human and administrative act of the Christian community. The purpose of ordination is for God and the church to endow and appoint some of the baptized for the public ministry of word and sacrament, which is essential for the existence, life and mission of the church. For churches with a broader concept of sacrament/sacramentality this understanding of ordination implies the application of the term "sacrament" to ordination. Also some churches which have used the term "sacrament" in a more limited way have shown themselves in their responses open to considering ordination, thus understood, as a "sacramental sign". Whether viewed as a sacrament or not ordination to the ministry is seen by all as serving the proclamation of the word and the administration of the sacraments. However, further dialogue and clarification will be necessary with regard to this issue both within the framework of the understanding of sacrament/sacramentality and especially also of ecclesiology.

d) In general, some Protestant responses have criticized the juxtaposition of baptism, eucharist and ministry in one single document as though this would put them all on the same level. In fact the three were put together because Faith and Order had decided to work on them as representing major church-dividing issues and at the same time essential elements of communion.

13. Mutual recognition of ordained ministries (M.51-55)

a) Critical comments in the responses to this part of the ministry section focused on M.53. Responses from Reformation and Free churches criticize what they regard as an imbalance between the steps proposed in M.53a and 53b: they are requested in M.53b to take a structured step (accepting the episcopal succession) while the "episcopal" churches are merely asked in M.53a to recognize a reality which the other churches believe they already possess. Such an act of full recognition, on the other hand, seems not to be possible at the moment for these churches as Roman Catholic and Orthodox responses indicate, for reasons of faith and ecclesial understanding.

b) Behind this criticism lies the fact that there is not an agreement on the necessity of the episcopal ministry and especially of episcopal succession in the church and on its necessity for the sake of mutual recognition of ministries. Such recognition is acknowledged by all to be an essential element in the unity we seek.

c) The paragraphs on mutual recognition in BEM are a consequence of the intention and thrust of the whole ministry section. However they could have indicated more clearly that recognition should not be seen as a single or isolated act, but rather as the outcome of a broader and more complex process. Such a process would include for example the factual acceptance of ministries as they are exercised in another church in serving the gospel of Jesus Christ through word and sacrament, the reality of the function of episkope in different forms, and the intention and forms of transmitting the ministry in continuity with apostolic times (cf. M.52). Essential to such a process would be the acknowledgment of an interrelationship between the understanding and reality of the ordained ministry and the understanding and reality of the church. The recognition of the ordained ministry and of the ecclesial character of a church are indissolubly and mutually related, as a number of responses affirm. It is in this wider ecclesiological framework that reflection on mutual recognition of ordained ministries should be further pursued.

V. Major Issues Demanding Further Study: Provisional Considerations

Introduction

Reflecting on the critical comments in the responses it became obvious that many of them were related to or expressions of more fundamental underlying issues. In a number of responses these issues were also directly mentioned as subjects for further work and, in some cases, as questions for the respective churches themselves. In the process leading up to this report three major issues were identified in which a number of specific issues needing further reflection are subsumed. They must remain on the Faith and Order agenda and will become an integral part of further work on ecumenical perspectives on ecclesiology. This work will draw on past studies in Faith and Order on Scripture and Tradition, sacraments/sacramentality and ecclesiology, on present Faith and Order projects on "The Unity of the Church and the Renewal of Human Community" and "Towards the Common Expression of the Apostolic Faith Today", and on results from bilateral dialogues. The considerations which follow are a first, preliminary attempt to relate insights and challenges from the responses to future work on these major issues, and to indicate some of the possible aspects and directions. This may serve also as a contribution to the ongoing discussion on BEM within and among the churches as well as to their other ecumenical tasks.

A. SCRIPTURE AND TRADITION

1. The issue of "Scripture and Tradition" has emerged as one of the main theological concerns among the churches responding to BEM. In the analytical description below of the responses we find it helpful to use the terminology which has developed in Faith and Order studies. "*Tradition*" with (a capital "T") refers to the comprehensive process of the transmis-

sion of the gospel in the power of the Holy Spirit from which the scriptures and also ecclesial traditions arise. The term "traditions" refers to these various ecclesial traditions which developed in the course of the centuries.

2. The statements on "Baptism, Eucharist and Ministry" were based on scriptural evidence. The use of the *scriptures* was generally and widely appreciated in the responses though a number of comments noted a lack of differentiation in the citations and sensed a lack of awareness of underlying exegetical issues. However a fundamental question is raised in the responses with regard to interpretations of *Tradition* and the use of *traditions* in the development of some of the theological arguments. Such issues were especially raised by the question addressed to the churches, to what extent they can recognize "the faith of the church through the ages" (cf. chap. III, paras 27 and 30-33). Some responses criticize that the scriptures have not always been allowed to function as the centre and norm of the faith, and there have also been questions why, when appeal was made to tradition, certain developments within the history of the church were apparently affirmed and not others and why certain periods were treated as more normative than others. It thus becomes clear that there is an overall need in the future work of Faith and Order for further clarification of the differences in regard to the roles which Scripture, Tradition and traditions actually play in the teaching of the churches and the roles which they should have in the shaping of ecumenical convergences in matters of doctrine.

1. Responses to the issue of "Scripture, Tradition and traditions"

3. In their responses all churches affirm the authority of Scripture. This is an important common basis. There are different ways, however, of describing the function of that authority in the process of Tradition and in relation to the traditions. Even where the priority of Scripture is affirmed, it can mean different things to different churches, e.g. the degree of "over-againstness" of Scripture to Tradition and traditions varies. These different views, as occurring in the responses to BEM, may be roughly grouped according to the following six types which illustrate different combinations and correlations between the three elements of Scripture, Tradition and traditions. It needs to be recognized that there is a certain artificiality about the delineation of six categories for they are not necessarily mutually exclusive and some responses relate to more than one type. References to specific responses are illustrative and do not necessarily suggest a confessional position.

Major Issues Demanding Further Study: Provisional Considerations 133

Nevertheless it is useful to set them out as indications of different positions and emphases which exist between and even within churches. This could stimulate a reconsideration of these positions and emphases by the churches, remind us of the complexity of the issues, and serve further work in Faith and Order on these issues raised at Montreal and discussed ever since. The goal of this work would be to develop convergent views on hermeneutical principles.

4. (a) By the first type, Scripture is considered to be the *only* authority for the life and the faith of the church (however, appeal is seldom made to *sola scriptura* without any awareness of the actual role of a tradition). "The faith of the church through the ages" is then identical with the "apostolic faith" attested in the scriptures, especially in the New Testament. As, for example, the Presbyterian Church of Ireland puts it: "The position of our church is that the sole authority for faith and life is Holy Scripture and that all subsequent traditions within the church are subject to this norm and criterion" (III.215). The Baptist Union of Denmark states: "We recognize in the document 'the faith of the Church throughout the ages' though we find this expression more a description of the creative power of the ecclesiastical tradition than the norm of confession which alone can be found in the canonical scriptures" (III.247). Or the Evangelical Lutheran Church of Hanover says: "We cannot but refer to the witness of the Scriptures" (IV.47). The exclusive appeal to Scripture, however, does not preclude the seeking of guidance from the living Christ and/or the Holy Spirit, the only warrant(s) of Tradition. In this case, "the faith of the church through the ages" is understood as primarily taking shape in the always actual *fides qua creditur*, and is not bound to particular articulations of faith.

5. (b) A second group would accept together with the priority of Scripture the Tradition of the "early" church as authoritative. The "constitutive period" for the formation of "the faith of the church through the ages" is variously defined as having lasted from the second to the eighth century. In any case, together with the priority of Scripture, the confessions/creeds of the ancient church, especially the Nicene-Constantinopolitan Creed, are received as authoritative interpretations of Scripture. To quote, for example, the Russian Orthodox Church's response: "The propriety of the methodology adopted by the Commission on Faith and Order... manifests itself in the fact that it is the faith of the church through the ages that has been made the criterion of evaluation, rather than a confessional approach of divided Christianity. What is implied here is the faith of one holy,

catholic and apostolic church, and the model for evaluation is supposed to be found in the faith and life of the early church of the seven ecumenical councils" (II.6).

6. (c) In a third group additional statements of faith are accepted together with the priority of Scripture and ancient creeds. "The faith of the church through the ages" is taken to mean the "faith according to the Scriptures" as it is understood by a specific confessional tradition claiming to be faithful to the criteria of the scriptures. As the Evangelical Church of Westphalia says: "The basis for our response is the question of the extent to which the biblical witness and the fundamental concern of the Reformation confessions as well as the latter's historical impact find expression" (IV.138).

7. (d) In a fourth type together with Scripture and Tradition a teaching office of the church, authoritatively interpreting Scripture and Tradition, is affirmed. "The faith of the church through the ages" is the apostolic faith as received in a particular tradition. While this tradition may be open to the insights and experiences of other churches, its authoritative teaching claims identity with the apostolic faith. The Roman Catholic response states clearly: "According to Catholic teaching (*Dei Verbum* 7-10) sacred Tradition and sacred scripture make up a single sacred deposit of the word of God which is entrusted to the church. They are bound closely together. Sacred scripture is the speech of God as it is put down in writing under the inspiration of the Holy Spirit. Tradition transmits in its entirety the word of God which has been entrusted to the apostles by Christ, in whom the entire revelation of God is summed up, and the Holy Spirit. It transmits it to the successors of the apostles, so that, enlightened by the Spirit of truth, they may faithfully preserve, expound and spread it abroad by their preaching. By adhering to it, the church remains always faithful to the teaching of the apostles, and to the gospel of Christ. Thus, in our view there must be a clear distinction made between the apostolic tradition, which obliges us because it is rooted in revelation, and the various traditions which may develop in local churches" (VI.7-8).

8. (e) In addition to Scripture and Tradition a fifth group emphasizes the place of reason as a valid criterion for the shaping of an authentic and living faith. The Anglican Church of Canada says: "... the method of the statement's theology is consistent with the accepted Anglican pattern of scripture, tradition and reason" (II.38). Some also emphasize the role of experience in the shaping of an authentic living Tradition (cf. United Methodist Church, USA, II.180).

9. (f) In a sixth group the basic perspective from which the issue of "Scripture and Tradition" is approached is that of the Faith and Order statement made in Montreal 1963: "The faith of the church through the ages" is interpreted as being synonymous with the dynamic understanding of "Tradition" according to the description of Montreal, including the faith of Israel as testified to in the Old Testament; it is the initiative of God's grace in the history of salvation, the gospel as the foundation of faith in every age. One example is the Lutheran Church in America which says: "They (i.e., Lutherans) place primary emphasis on the gospel as witnessed to in Scripture. The gospel is the foundation of the faith in every age, including the biblical period, the apostolic age or the second, third and sixteenth centuries" (I.34; cf. Church of England, III.38).

10. Whatever their views on the relations between Scripture, Tradition and traditions, most responses show an awareness of the hermeneutical problems involved in the formulation of the question concerning "the faith of the church through the ages" in the BEM texts. Some of them state those problems in the form of critical remarks or proposals for further study (e.g., United Reformed Church in the United Kingdom, I.104; Church of Sweden, II.124; Evangelical Lutheran Church of Finland, III.125; Melanesian Council of Churches, V.184; Roman Catholic Church, VI.8,27,32).

2. The Faith and Order debate on Scripture, Tradition and church from Montreal to BEM

11. The discussion on these matters should be read in the light of the ecumenical debate on the hermeneutical question since the Fourth World Conference on Faith and Order in Montreal 1963, section II on "Scripture, Tradition and Traditions".[1] This was followed up by Faith and Order work on "The Significance of the Hermeneutical Problem for the Ecumenical Movement" since 1964,[2] on "Councils and the Ecumenical Movement",[3] on "The Authority of the Bible",[4] on "Towards Common

---

[1] P.C. Rodger & L. Vischer eds, *The Fourth World Conference on Faith and Order*, London, SCM, 1964.
[2] Cf. *New Directions in Faith and Order*, reports, minutes and documents of the Commission meeting in Bristol 1967, Geneva, WCC, 1968.
[3] Studies of the WCC, No. 5, Geneva, WCC, 1968.
[4] Cf. *Faith and Order, Louvain, 1971*, study reports and documents, Geneva, 1971; E. Flesseman-van Leer ed., *The Bible: Its Authority and Interpretation in the Ecumenical Movement*, Geneva, WCC, 1980.

Ways of Teaching and Decision-Making"[5] and since 1978 on "Towards the Common Expression of the Apostolic Faith Today".[6]

12. The Montreal statement on "Scripture, Tradition and Traditions" represented a remarkable point of convergence: "... we exist as Christians by the Tradition of the gospel, testified in Scripture, transmitted in and by the church, through the power of the Holy Spirit. Tradition taken in this sense is actualized in the preaching of the word, in the administration of the sacraments and worship, in Christian teaching and theology, and in mission and witness to Christ by the lives of the members of the church."[7]

13. This formulation tried to give expression to a common ecumenical conviction about the inner relation between (1) the preceding prophetic and apostolic Tradition, (2) the scriptures which emerged from this as their normative witness (3), the successive ecclesial traditions, which are obligated to proclaim and explain the Tradition of the gospel, testified in Scripture as the primary instrument of the gospel. Though the transmission process as a whole is seen as operative through the power of the Holy Spirit, the hermeneutical problem of the relation between Scripture and authoritative ecclesial traditions or between those traditions and Tradition (i.e. the transmission of the gospel as a whole including Scripture) was not made sufficiently clear at that time. Montreal only listed the various positions within the ecumenical spectrum,[8] much along lines similar to those now manifest in the responses. It could not go beyond a mere juxtaposition of three factors in the transmission process:

— the preceding events and testimonies leading to Scripture;
— the scriptures themselves; and
— the ecclesial preaching and teaching.

No criteria were offered in Montreal, only questions asked:

— "How can we distinguish between traditions embodying the true Tradition and merely human traditions?"[9]

---

[5] Cf. *Sharing in One Hope*, Commission on Faith and Order, Bangalore, 1978, Geneva, WCC, 1978.
[6] Cf. *Towards a Confession of the Common Faith*, Geneva, WCC, 1980; *Confessing One Faith*, Geneva, WCC, 1987.
[7] *The Fourth World Conference...*, *op. cit.*, section II, para. 45.
[8] *Ibid.*, para. 53.
[9] *Ibid.*, para. 48.

— "How can we overcome the situation in which we all read Scripture in the light of our own traditions?"[10]
— "Does not the ecumenical situation demand that we search for the Tradition by re-examining our own particular traditions?"[11]

14. The ongoing debate within Faith and Order resulted in 1978 in a common conviction, formulated in Bangalore: "Before the church performs acts of teaching, she exists and lives. Her existence and her life are the work of the Triune God who calls her into being and sustains her as his people, the body of Christ, the fellowship of the faithful in the Spirit. The authority of the church has its ground in this *datum* of her being. The whole church teaches by what she is, when she is living according to the gospel... We obey the truth because we have been persuaded by it."[12]

15. Two things are implied here: (a) The ecclesial character of the transmission process: Tradition, Scripture, church, cannot be treated as separate phenomena. There is no Tradition without concrete human traditions, there is no Scripture without a community of believers; there is no church without the God-given Tradition or without the living word of God in the scriptures. (b) The whole process of transmission stands under the criterion of faithful witness to the gospel, preached by the apostles, of God's free grace and truth. "For the post-apostolic church the appeal to the Tradition received from the apostles became the criterion. As this Tradition was embodied in the apostolic writings, it became natural to use those writings as an authority for determining where the true Tradition was to be found. In the midst of all tradition, these early records of divine revelation have a special basic value, because of their apostolic character."[13]

16. Thus it is not only the texts of Tradition, like scriptures or the creeds or the sacramental forms of the early church, but also the living word of God, Christ incarnate, and the life-giving Spirit, who lead the church into the truth. The Tradition means a permanent dialogue of the church with Christ, an unbroken communion with divine life, a permanent presence of the Holy Spirit.[14] The post-apostolic Tradition, however, in its diverse forms of teaching with regard to faith and

---

[10] *Ibid.*, para. 54.
[11] *Ibid.*, para. 55.
[12] *Sharing in One Hope*, op. cit., p.258.
[13] *The Fourth World Conference...*, op. cit., para. 49.
[14] Cf. G. Florovsky, *Orthodoxy*, Geneva, 1960, p.60.

practices of life and worship, is always obligated to be a faithful reflection of the apostolic truth and of the continuous intention of faith (cf. M.52). It is "interpretative" and "receptive", based on apostolic faith as its source.

17. The way has been opened towards an ecumenical convergence on hermeneutical principles by pointing to the Tradition as *paradosis*, as a gift to be received and transmitted. The scriptures as a unique, divine gift of grace to the people of God are themselves both the fruit of the prophetic and apostolic tradition and the seed and impulse of the ongoing process of transmission and reception. This process is seen as a continuing, future-oriented and indeed eschatological, dynamic and living event. The results of the historical-critical method in exegesis had already opened up the hermeneutical debate about Scripture and Tradition before Montreal. Since then other developments in modern hermeneutics have suggested perspectives that may also be useful in continuing work in Faith and Order on this question.

18. After Montreal research into the social, cultural and political contexts of the ministry of Jesus Christ and the life of the early church of the New Testament and of the early patristic era was able to add new insights about diversity and unity of traditions, creeds and liturgies of the early church. And modern semiotic approaches called our attention to the specific functions of the narrative shape and style of Jewish and Christian literature.

19. The ecumenical dialogue itself can be seen as a unique opportunity where the hermeneutical process takes place under the commonly acknowledged authority of God's word. The paradosis of the gospel is received within a continuous re-reading *(relecture)*, re-reception and reappropriation of the narrative of God's salvation.

3. Tradition, Scripture and the church in BEM

20. Following that same line of thought, the preface to BEM states: "On the way towards their goal of visible unity, however, the churches will have to pass through various stages. They have been blessed anew through listening to each other and jointly returning to the primary sources, namely 'the Tradition of the Gospel testified in Scripture, transmitted in and by the Church through the power of the Holy Spirit' (Faith and Order World Conference, Montreal, 1963). In leaving behind the hostilities of the past, the churches have begun to discover many promising convergences in their shared convictions and perspectives. These convergences give assurance that despite much diversity in

theological expression the churches have much in common in their understanding of the faith. The resultant text aims to become part of a faithful and sufficient reflection of the common Christian Tradition on essential elements of Christian communion. In the process of growing together in mutual trust, the churches must develop these doctrinal convergences step by step, until they are finally able to declare together that they are living in communion with one another in continuity with the apostles and the teachings of the universal Church" (p.ix).

21. It was on the basis of this theological understanding of a given, common apostolic Tradition and of a received, partially shared and growing universal communion, that the first question, put before the churches, was phrased like this: "The extent to which your church can recognize in this text *the faith of the church through the ages.*" Its aim was to broaden the scope of the particular teaching of any given tradition towards the wider reality of a common Christian Tradition, especially the permanent witness of the scriptures throughout Christian history, from which the divided churches would draw, through the ecumenical movement, the opportunities for renewal and enrichment of their understanding of sacraments and ministry. Its aim was also to direct the attention of the churches to their ecumenism-in-time, and to the dynamic idea of apostolic Tradition.

22. The same understanding has led to the description of the leading idea of "apostolic Tradition" in the ministry text: "In the Creed, the Church confesses itself to be apostolic. The Church lives in continuity with the apostles and their proclamation. The same Lord who sent the apostles continues to be present in the Church. The Spirit keeps the Church in the apostolic tradition until the fulfilment of history in the Kingdom of God. Apostolic tradition in the Church means continuity in the permanent characteristics of the Church of the apostles: witness to the apostolic faith, proclamation and fresh interpretation of the Gospel, celebration of baptism and the eucharist, the transmission of ministerial responsibilities, communion in prayer, love, joy and suffering, service to the sick and the needy, unity among the local churches and sharing the gifts which the Lord has given to each" (M.34 and comm.).

23. Keywords in this understanding of "apostolic Tradition" are:
— *apostolic continuity* (in proclamation, mission, interpretation of the gospel, celebration of the sacraments, transmission of ministerial responsibilities);

— *community* (sharing in the gifts of God, in prayer, service, unity); and
— *fulfilment of history in the kingdom of God*.[15]

24. This understanding of Tradition goes beyond the scope of the Montreal debate. The report on "Scripture, Tradition and Traditions" had no intrinsic relation to the other findings of Montreal in section I on "The Church in the Purpose of God";[16] section III on "The Redemptive Work of Christ and the Ministry of His Church";[17] section IV on "Worship and the Oneness of Christ's Church";[18] section V on "'All in Each Place': The Process of Growing Together".[19] It was precisely in drawing from these sections of Montreal and relating them to the idea of a living ecclesial Tradition that Faith and Order developed the convergence process represented in BEM.

25. "Tradition" *(paradosis)* and "communion" *(koinonia)* intend both past and present: there is need to discern a continuity of the apostolic faith and of the believing community in history; there needs to be also a contemporary solidarity of local churches united in faith and reconciled in a universal communion. In the commentary to M.34 the content of ecclesial Tradition is described as a "transmission process", which

---

[15] *"Continuity"*, e.g., in preface ix-x; B.1-6,8-10,19; E.1-9,11 (in communion with all the saints and martyrs), 13-14,19-21,25 (the church's participation in God's mission to the world), 29; M.1-6,8-12,15 (the authority of the ordained minister is rooted in Jesus Christ), 19-23,29 (bishops as ministers of continuity), 34-38 (on apostolic tradition and succession), 39 (ordination:... to continue the mission of the apostles), 52 ("churches in ecumenical conversations can recognize their respective ordained ministries if they are mutually assured of their intention to transmit the ministry of word and sacrament in continuity with apostolic times"), 53(b) ("in faithful continuity with the apostolic faith and mission"; "... continuity with the church of the apostles").

"Community", e.g. in B.6,7,18,15; E.10,17 (community of the new covenant), 19-21,26,29 (connection of the local community with other local communities in the universal church); M.1-6,8 (focus of unity), 11 (to assemble and guide the dispersed people of God, 12 (to build up the community in Christ), 13 (to build up the body of Christ), 21 (episkope: focus of unity), 23 (to safeguard the unity of the body), 26-27 (communal dimension of ministry), 29 (relate the Christian community in their area to the wider church, and the universal church to their community); 34 (unity among the local churches); 38 (unity of the whole church), 54-55 (overcoming differences, recognition of ministries).

"Fulfilment in the kingdom of God", e.g., in B.3-5,7,9-10,19,21; E.1-4,6-7,13-14,17-18,20,22-26; M.1-6,8,11,34 (the Spirit keeps the church in the apostolic tradition until the fulfilment of history in the kingdom of God).

[16] Esp. paras 19-23.

[17] Esp. paras 83-87; 90-98.

[18] Esp. para. 108, 111 (on baptism) and 116-117 (on eucharist).

[19] Esp. para. 154 on worship and sacraments.

relates the actual church and its ministries to the gospel and to "the saving words and acts of Jesus Christ which constitute the life of the Church". In the opening paragraphs and at many other places in BEM (e.g., in M.1-6,8-14,15-16,19-23) this same basic idea of Tradition as transmission of the salvific gifts of Christ in and by the church through the power of the Holy Spirit has been expressed. Reference to this process of transmission is found also in the commentaries, e.g., to B.13,18,21, M.18,39.

4. Suggestions for future work

26. The positions taken in the responses relative to Scripture, Tradition and traditions as described, have definite implications for renewal and change within the various churches with regard to faith and practice of baptism, Lord's supper and ministry. Examples are: the baptism of infants or adult believers, the relationship between apostolic tradition and episcopal succession, the acceptance or rejection of the threefold ministry of bishop, presbyter and deacon, teaching authority of the church or the ordination of women. The primacy of one or some patriarchal see(s) could be still another example.

27. Such questions cannot be solved on the basis of clarification of terms only. Trusting in God's promise to keep them in the truth, each and every church has ways and means for discerning and judging truth according to various structures of decision-making and teaching authority. All churches believe that they receive the truth of the gospel as a gift from God through Tradition *(paradosis)*. In this sense they do not "possess" the truth, but are guided and corrected by the truth. They also believe that they may grow into a fuller understanding of that truth and that they are obliged to find credible expressions of their faith and life in Christ who is the truth.

28. Future work on Scripture, Tradition, traditions and the church would be helped by the insight that the expression "the faith of the church through the ages", implies a certain theological interpretation of Tradition as an ecclesial, dynamic event. This would include two essential criteria for discerning and expressing the truth of the Christian faith:

— The first criterion is that of *faithfulness* to the witness of prophets, apostles and martyrs and its crystallization in the scriptures, which are the authoritative expression of the word of God for all humanity. This criterion reflects the definite will to act and to confess according to the

faith of the ecclesial community, led by its teachers and pastors in the power of the Holy Spirit. This criterion presupposes a context of shared faith in a common Tradition and a readiness to listen to the voices of past Tradition in order to respond to new challenges in new contexts.
— The second criterion is that of *conciliarity*, i.e., of being attentive to the present witness of all the local churches within the universal church as a conciliar community. The problem here is the churches' broken conciliar life itself. The ecumenical movement and reception processes like that of BEM are only a preliminary and incomplete prefiguration for a genuine conciliarity.

Both criteria still raise the question of the authority of Scripture and how it is to be interpreted. BEM leads us to believe that a critical reading of the scriptures has given us the opportunity of overcoming some of the ecclesiastical controversies of the past (compare para. 25).

29. But now, as becomes clear from the responses to BEM, churches are beginning to realize that regardless of their particular confessional and ecclesiological traditions, it is essential for them to be in relationship with one another, learning from the insights and experiences of others in order to reach unity and fulfill their mission. Not only is it true "that the Spirit may well speak to one church through the insights of another" (M.54), but perhaps even more, every church has to be aware of its fundamental task of love (John 13) and reconciliation (Matt. 18:22) and of its fundamental inheritance in the one divine initiative of grace in Israel (Rom. 11).

30. Faith and Order should reflect on the biblical foundation of this dynamic understanding of Tradition, in order to integrate the Old Testament into the concept of Tradition. In so doing there should be an attempt to show how the signs and institutions of the covenant in Israel of old, were fulfilled in and through the ministry of Jesus so that they can now contribute to "the preaching of the gospel until the ends of the oikoumene" (Matt. 24:14).

31. The life and mission of the church in manifold contexts calls for permanent renewal in the Holy Spirit. Any continuing reflection upon Scripture, Tradition and traditions and the church should take place in relation to concrete issues on the basis of the obedience to the truth of the living Christ granted to us under the guidance of the Holy Spirit in all generations to come. Thus, Tradition will not only reflect the past but becomes a future-oriented reality.

B. SACRAMENT AND SACRAMENTALITY

1. Mystery, sacrament and sacramentality

The three parts of the Lima text concentrate respectively on baptism, eucharist and ministry in the specific particularity of each of the three. In their responses, the churches have raised several questions concerning the sacramental features which the three may have in common. The questions are often phrased in terms of the understanding, role and place of "sacrament" and "sacramentality" in the BEM text. Behind such questions lie different understandings of sacrament and sacramentality. In part, the problems are terminological: the Eastern churches always used the term "mystery", which in the New Testament designates principally the saving purpose of God revealed in Christ; the Western church used "sacrament" together with "mystery", though the term brought other connotations with it from the legal world and allowed some of the associations of "mystery" to be overshadowed; the churches of the Reformation maintained the term sacrament though with different understandings and most of them limited it to those rites they saw as instituted and ordained by the Lord Jesus in the scriptures. Another request in the responses of the churches is for a clarification of the notion of "sacramentality". The following description is now proposed and is also meant as a framework and point of reference for the more detailed comments which then follow.

2. The history of salvation and sacramentality

The covenant of God with Israel is celebrated, according to the witness of the Old Testament, in manifold signs of that covenant, which are understood as prefigurations of the signs of the new covenant. In line with this heritage, the New Testament and the Tradition of the church have developed a sacramental view of the history of salvation which could be described as follows:

> In the incarnation, life, death and resurrection of Jesus Christ, God has communicated effectively the mystery of his saving love to the world. Through the power of the Holy Spirit, the risen Christ continues this saving action of God by being present and active in our midst. For this purpose God continues to act through human persons, through their words, signs and actions, together with elements of creation. Thus God communicates to the faithful, and through their witness to the world, his saving promise and grace. Those who hear

and receive in faith and trust this gracious action of God are thereby liberated from their captivity to sin and transformed in their lives. Those who receive this gift, respond to it in thanksgiving and praise and are brought into a *koinonia* with the Holy Trinity and with each other and are sent to proclaim the gospel to the whole world. Through this sacramental action, communicated through words, signs and actions, this community, the church, is called, equipped and sent, empowered and guided by the Holy Spirit to witness to God's reconciling and recreating love in a sinful and broken world. And so all who in faith long for fullness of life in Christ may experience the first-fruits of God's kingdom — present and yet to be fully accomplished in a new-heaven and earth.

Such a sacramental understanding of the history of salvation could help to overcome some of the difficulties expressed in the responses.

3. The mystery of Christ and the sacraments

The process by which particular events in the life of the church came to be called "mysteries" and "sacraments" in the light of the general conception of "mystery" in the New Testament, is still under discussion. A biblical justification of the sacramental terminology seems possible only if one starts with the notion of "mystery", which comprises both Christ and his church (Col. 1:26f., 2:2; Eph. 3:9ff., a.o.). Within the divine plan of salvation, already revealed in Jesus Christ, the ecclesial actions, later called sacraments, are each in a specific way communicating the saving presence of Christ in his church. They do so as signs of the new covenant and as the first-fruits and the instalment of the Holy Spirit.[1]

4. The agent of the sacraments

When the risen Lord commanded his followers to teach and to baptize in the name of the Father, the Son and the Holy Spirit, he assured them that he would be with them to the end of the age (Matt. 28:28-30). Equally it is the Lord himself who commanded and commands his disciples to eat the bread and drink the cup in remembrance of him (1 Cor. 11:23-26). When BEM says "baptism is..." or "the eucharist does...", the real subject of the sentence is the Triune God: "In baptism/the eucharist, God through Christ in the Holy Spirit..." It is thus clear, and this was also the intention of BEM, that the church does not exist or act without its

---

[1] Cf. Groupe des Dombes, *L'Esprit Saint, l'Eglise et les sacrements,* Taizé, 1979.

head, Jesus Christ. The church is neither independent of its divine master nor do baptism and eucharist have their role and efficacy in themselves independently of God's action. Indeed all ministries and actions of God's people are dependent on the Lord for their origin and sustenance.

5. Sacraments and faith

Integral to an understanding of sacraments is the fact that God's action in the church in baptism and the Lord's supper as well as in the exercise of the churches' various ministries require a response of faith — faith being in itself a gift nourished by the Holy Spirit. This leaves unanswered the question about the status of a sacramental act which may have no discernable relation to personal faith (either before, concurrent with or subsequent to the act). Churches understand and express differently how God's sacramental gift and the believer's faith relate to each other. All agree however that God's gift is directed towards evoking such a response.

6. Word and sacrament

Word and sacrament are indivisibly linked in communicating God's saving action in Jesus Christ, the word made flesh, the mystery of the kingdom of God becoming present among us. In baptism and the eucharist both the proclamation of God's word and the participation in God's sacramental action are inseparable; together they communicate God's grace. Thus, through word and sacrament we participate in the death of Christ and in his resurrection and are liberated from the powers of sin and are made a new creation. Using the term sacramental in a general sense, i.e., referring to God's salvific action in history, the proclamation of the word is a sacramental action just as the celebration of baptism and supper are an event of God's word. When the inseparability of word and sacrament is accepted, there is liberty to acknowledge the particular functions of each within and for the Christian community and also their critical role over against inadequate forms of worship and life.

7. Sacrament and sign

In any future study on sacraments and sacramentality, the issue of sacraments as signs should be studied (cf. "Clarifications", A.6). The historical controversies on this point have arisen on the basis of different philosophical interpretations of "sign" *(signum)* in East and West and between the churches of the West themselves concerning the relation between the signified reality *(res)* and the mediating sign *(signum)*. More research could be done on the relation of the sacraments to the biblical notion of "semeion", the idea of the sign of the covenant (cf. para. 2) and the narrative structure of the prophetic sign-actions of the prophets of Israel and in the ministry of Jesus.[2]

8. Church and sacraments

By God's saving grace through word and sacrament the church becomes church, i.e., the body of Christ under the lordship of Christ. As a human reality, however, the church is marked by the vicissitudes of history and by the sinfulness of its members, who constantly stand in need of forgiveness and renewal. Nevertheless God's action in baptism, eucharist and preaching as well as God's action in the churches' various ministries remains effective and powerful despite human weakness: "We have this treasure in earthen vessels to show that the transcendent power belongs to God and not to us" (2 Cor. 4:7).

9. Sacraments in Christian life

Many responses to BEM have welcomed the references to the ethical implications of the sacraments, and some ask for further clarification and study. It is, therefore, suggested that:

a) The cosmological dimension of the sacraments be further studied, taking into account the material elements used in the sacraments (representing creation and human labour, and the fact that the sacraments touch and are also touched by all aspects of human life. The sacraments, as instances of God's redemptive activity, have an exemplary and critical function towards the use and abuse of nature. They contribute to the transformation of the world according to God's purpose for humanity and creation, to be ultimately fulfilled at the end of the ages.

b) The social dimension of the sacraments should also be studied further. Such a study should take into account St Paul's critique of discrimination and division in the community (1 Cor. 11). The study should also apply the concept and reality of the new community created by word and sacrament in the church both to individual problems like loneliness, despair and hopelessness, and also to the social problems of a divided humanity such as riches and poverty, oppression, totalitarianism, militarism, discrimination on account of race, sex, ethnic or religious identity.

---

[2] Cf. Groupe des Dombes, *L'Esprit Saint, L'Eglise et les sacrements*; Faith and Order Study on the Unity of the Church and the Renewal of Human Community.

10. Non-sacramental communities

Within the wide horizon of God's abundant gifts of grace, communities which do not practise baptism and eucharist experience God's grace and several of them develop an affirmative articulation of the general sacramental dimension of life within the Christian faith. In this connection the affirmation of the 1963 Montreal World Conference should be remembered that "we gladly acknowledge that some who do not observe these rites share in the spiritual experience of life in Christ" (p.72). The acknowledgment of God's grace being present and active beyond the sacraments ought not, however, to lead to relativizing the necessity and centrality of sacraments together with the proclamation of the word by those churches which are committed to Christ's institution of them. Christ's command to baptize and to celebrate the supper in his memory should strengthen for these churches an appreciation of the sacramental quality of the whole of life.

C. PERSPECTIVES ON ECCLESIOLOGY IN THE CHURCHES' RESPONSES

1. Ecclesiological aspects in the responses

1. The search for Christian unity implies the search for common ecumenical perspectives on ecclesiology. This need is strongly underlined by the analysis of the responses to BEM which reveal many different presuppositions but also convergences regarding the nature of the church. These convergences are shared by a number of churches, although with different emphases. Especially in the innumerable comments on specific points in BEM as well as in more general statements, various understandings of church are implied; the consequences of divisive issues of the past are still evident; and problems arising from new contextual situations are highlighted, such as social, geo-political challenges through the world, changed attitudes regarding the status of women and their participation in the life of the church, and interaction with people of other faiths.

2. In the light of the Lima document, to which Christian churches throughout the world are responding, new momentum is given to the search for common perspectives on ecclesiology. In the responses to BEM we find positive references to a number of ecclesiological aspects which could contribute to future work of Faith and Order on ecclesiology. Many churches emphasize the corporate nature of the sacraments which express and build up the communal character of the church on all levels of

its life. Many also welcome a Christocentric and Trinitarian perspective for the understanding of the church, which implies a corrective for an ecclesiology which is primarily concerned with the church as a historical institution. Numerous responses find in the convergences on baptism and the eucharist possibilities for a common vision of the church on the basis of an already existing, albeit imperfect, unity. Many churches also emphasize the ethical implications of the sacraments and their missionary and eschatological character which relate ecclesiology to the challenge and promise of God's kingdom for the sake of the world. The fact that churches are prepared to learn from each other is already a sign of their growing communion with each other.

3. Within these common perspectives, however, certain areas remain in need of further study. These include the following: the role and place of the church in God's saving action — especially in relation to the sacraments; the rootedness of the church in the faith of Israel and the covenants of God with Israel; the essential characteristics or marks of the church; the relationship of the ordained ministry to the priesthood of the whole people of God; the ministries of women; forms of the ordained and lay ministries; apostolic Tradition and episcopal succession; the teaching authority and decision-making processes; the relationship of the local and universal dimensions of the church; the service of unity among the churches at a universal level with its implications for teaching and decision-making.

4. Because of issues such as these many responses to BEM requested *that ecclesiology be made a major study in future Faith and Order work.* Such an ecclesiology in an ecumenical perspective must take into account the various ideas of the church which reflect the churches' different self-understanding and their views on the nature of the church and its unity. It also requires the search for basic ecclesiological principles, which could provide common perspectives for the churches' different ecclesiologies and serve as a framework for their convergence. These principles could be appropriately applied in different contextual situations in the life of the churches.

2. The role of the church in God's saving purpose

5. As the people of God and the body of Christ, the church is built up by the word *(creatura verbi divini)* and enlivened by the Holy Spirit. The Triune God constantly constitutes and nourishes the church through the preaching of the gospel and the celebration of baptism and holy communion. Receiving its existence from God, the church is in turn used by God

for the furtherance of God's saving action, through word and sacrament, to new generations and to the whole world. This instrumental role of the church may be expressed in various ways: servants of the word, stewards of the mysteries of God, ministers of Christ, witnesses to the Spirit. All the ministries of the people of God, according to their particular gifts and responsibilities, share in this task, just as they are all dependent on God for their origin and sustenance.

6. In speaking about any role and activity of the church, one should never forget the initiative of God's grace. This initiative of grace, beginning with Israel *(qahal JHWH)* and continued and fulfilled in Jesus Christ *(ekklesia tou Christou)* is intended for all people. It has, therefore, taken the form of a historical movement through the power of the Holy Spirit towards unity and community among human beings on the basis of their reconciliation with God in Christ and across all boundaries that otherwise separate people and nations. Thus, the church is called to serve the gospel of reconciliation which brings "justice and peace and joy in the Holy Spirit" (Rom. 14:17).

7. This divine-human mystery, which is the church, bears witness to the freedom of God and calls for the responsibility of human beings. The Holy Spirit of God uses human beings and their activity in his creative and recreative work which is aimed at transforming and strengthening sinful, violent humans towards solidarity and service, witness and prayer, until this human activity is ultimately fulfilled in the praise and adoration of God "in spirit and in truth" (John 4:23).

8. The covenant community of all who were united through faith and worship of the one God within the life of one particular people has been opened up beyond the boundaries of this people by Jesus' death and resurrection. Thus, the life of the crucified and risen Christ has become, through the outpouring of the Holy Spirit, the source for a new, eschatological communion of human beings from all nations (Rom. 11:11), who are united by their faith in the God of Israel, who in Jesus Christ revealed himself to be the creator and redeemer of all humanity. Consequently, it has been the continuing concern of the apostolic tradition and mission to bring together from among all nations the servants of God into one, holy, catholic and apostolic church.

3. *Koinonia*

9. In the responses to BEM the churches have referred to this understanding of God's presence and action within the church in terms of *koinonia* (communion/participation/fellowship). The notion of *koinonia*

is currently being given serious attention by many churches and also in a number of bilateral conversations between churches. It is suggested that it be pursued seriously in Faith and Order work towards a convergent vision on ecclesiology, although the notion of *koinonia* should not be regarded as the only possible approach.

10. *Koinonia* in the life of the Father, the Son and the Holy Spirit (cf. John 14:17; 1 John 1:2-10; 2 Pet. 1:4; 1 Cor. 1:9; 2 Cor. 13:13) is the life centre of all who confess Jesus Christ as Lord and Saviour. They share and participate in the gospel and in the apostolic faith, in suffering and in service (2 Cor. 8:4; Rom. 15:26; Acts 2:32). This *koinonia* is lived in Christ through baptism (Rom. 6) and the eucharist (1 Cor. 11) and in the community with its pastors and guides (Heb. 13). *Koinonia* means in addition the participation in the holy things of God and the communion of the saints of all times and places (*communio sanctorum* in the double sense of the word). Each local Christian community is related in *koinonia* with all other local Christian communities with whom it shares the same faith. In this *koinonia* they live the catholicity of the church. To say it with the words of the Lima document: "Witness to the apostolic faith, proclamation and fresh interpretation of the gospel, celebration of baptism and the eucharist, the transmission of ministerial responsibilities, communion in prayer, love, joy and suffering, service to the sick and the needy, unity among the local churches and sharing the gifts which the Lord has given to each" (M.34). Such a *koinonia* is not an inward-looking group of believers, but a missionary community sent into the world to bear witness to God's love for humanity and creation.

11. This general description of *koinonia* which all may be able to hold, could be further developed with the help of different key conceptions and images which have been especially emphasized by different Christian traditions. Together they could contribute in a complementary way to an ecumenically oriented ecclesiology of *koinonia*.

a) The church as gift of the word of God (creatura verbi)

12. The *koinonia* of the church is centred and grounded in the word of God testified in the scriptures, incarnated in Jesus Christ and visible among us through the living voice of the gospel in preaching, in sacraments and in service. All church institutions, forms of ministry, liturgical expressions and methods of mission should be submitted to the word of God and tested by it. The *pleroma* of God's creative word is never exhausted in the churches' institutions.

b) The church as mystery or sacrament of God's love for the world

13. The church as *koinonia* is the church of the living God (1 Tim. 3:15), not a human association only. It lives in permanent communion with God the Father through Jesus Christ in the Holy Spirit and is not merely the historical product of Jesus' ministry. Because of its intimate relation with Christ himself as the head of the body, the church is to be confessed according to the apostolic faith as one, holy, catholic and apostolic. Therefore the visible organizational structures of the church must always be seen in the light of God's gifts of salvation in Christ. The word and the sacraments of Jesus Christ are forms of God's real and saving presence for the world. As such they express the church's participation in the mystery of Christ and are inseparable from it.

c) The church as the pilgrim people of God

14. A third aspect of the understanding of the church as *koinonia* stresses the provisional and incomplete character of the church in its present form, its hope and despair, its suffering and compassion, its shame and glory, its being still a mixed reality of sinners and saints. The church is a community of justified sinners in search of the kingdom of God, struggling as they serve the world to be obedient to the commands and promises of Christ as expressed in the sermon on the mount. It is a community of pilgrims who have already received a foretaste of that fulfilment for which they are longing.

d) The church as servant and prophetic sign of God's coming kingdom

15. The church is also a servant people for God's coming kingdom, "the sign held up before the nations". As a first-fruit of the kingdom the church takes sides with the weak, the poor and the alienated. This is for the sake of involving all its members in a personal appeal to seek first of all the kingdom of God by being itself, as a collective whole, an instrument for the liberation of people in distress. An ecumenically conceived ecclesiology, therefore, must not be self-centred, triumphalistic or complacent, but should direct the churches' service to the world (M.1-5), to justice, peace and the integrity of creation.

16. Since all these concepts and images belong to the common biblical heritage and are found in the apostolic tradition there is hope that in the future work of Faith and Order on ecumenical perspectives of ecclesiology these complementary approaches will lead to a convergent vision on the nature, unity and mission of the church.

Part Three

Appendices

APPENDIX I

Baptism, Eucharist and Ministry: the Continuing Call to Unity

A Statement by the Faith and Order Commission
Addressed to the Churches, Budapest, August 1989

I. Moving into unity

1. The Faith and Order Commission, a servant of the churches, meeting in Budapest in August 1989, thanks the churches for the serious manner in which they have studied and responded to *Baptism, Eucharist and Ministry*. The responses received have been closely studied by the Commission, as will be responses still to come. The responses have been published in six volumes. The Commission has now prepared a comprehensive summary and evaluation of the process and the responses to date in *Baptism, Eucharist and Ministry 1982-1989: Report on the Process and Responses*, to be published in 1990. The Commission rejoices at the manifold evidence that BEM is not only stimulating discussion and dialogue between the churches, but is also enabling them to grow closer together in their life, worship and mission. The Commission reaffirms its commitment to serve the churches on the pilgrimage to visible unity.

2. When the Faith and Order Commission of the World Council of Churches completed its work on the *Baptism, Eucharist and Ministry* text in January 1982 in Lima, Peru, no one foresaw the interest which the BEM statement would evoke in the Christian community. No one envisaged the impact which it would have within and among churches of such diverse historical origins and such varying traditions. This fruit of many years of ecumenical discussion has become the most widely distributed, translated, and discussed ecumenical text in modern times. Some 450,000 copies translated into 31 languages have been studied in a huge variety of situations around the world. Over a thousand written reactions have so far been published. Never before have more than 180 churches reached out to each other by responding officially to an ecumenical document. Never before have so many from theological

faculties, confessional families, ecumenical groups, local congregations, and discussion groups of lay and ordained persons joined together in studying the same modern ecumenical document. In their willingness to understand and approach this task in a positive spirit, all have offered a sign of commitment to our common movement towards the visible unity of the church for which Christ prayed and which has its deepest roots in the communion of the Trinity.

3. For all this we invite you to join us in giving thanks to God.

II. Advances in unity

4. The churches' response to BEM has created a new ecumenical situation. BEM came at a moment when the churches were looking for a new way forward towards unity. It spoke to issues close to the life and faith of people in our communions. It expressed broad convergence on basic Christian affirmations and revealed sometimes surprising agreements.

5. In many churches' responses to the BEM document this convergence was affirmed. We find general gratitude in the responses for the Trinitarian basis of the Lima statement — a firm agreement that baptism, eucharist and ministry are all rightly understood as enacted and enabled by God in the unity of Father, Son and Holy Spirit. Virtually all agree on the Trinitarian shape of baptism, that by God's grace and power the person baptized is incorporated into Christ's body and anointed by the Holy Spirit. There is growing agreement on the centrality of the eucharist or Lord's supper in the life of the church. This celebration always includes the proclamation of God's word together with the supper as one action in which Christ is present. In this celebration, not only Jesus' last supper with the disciples but the whole of God's creating, redeeming and sanctifying action through Christ is recalled. The churches agreed in affirming BEM's approach to ministry in terms of our shared baptism and the calling of the whole people of God. There was common approval for the description of the responsibilities of the ordained ministry and for the emphasis on the personal, collegial, and communal dimensions of the exercise of ministry. For all the sections of the text, the churches offered general affirmation of the strong confession of the ethical dimension in the church's worship which links it with living faithfulness in the world. They affirmed the clear grounding of all these aspects of the BEM text in the holy scriptures.

6. We acknowledge with joy that BEM has taken a place in the internal life of many churches, becoming part of the process by which some teach and pass on the apostolic faith. Churches are allowing BEM to stimulate

them to critical discussion of their own traditions and practices. They show a willingness to change perceptions of other communions' beliefs, worship and practices. For many churches BEM has become the occasion for specific commitments to renewal and enrichment in their own faith, practice, ecumenical relations, and missionary witness.

7. As a convergence statement composed by people from separated churches and diverse traditions, BEM calls neither for surrender, nor compromise, nor total acceptance, and certainly not for ambiguity or confusion. It calls rather for common affirmations by divided churches struggling towards universal communion. BEM treats three subjects but with one theme: the visible unity of Christ's body. In their responses the churches have engaged with each other at a new level. And they have offered each other a basis for new relationships. Thus the process of response is itself a visible sign of our movement into unity.

8. For all this we invite you to join us in giving thanks to God.

III. Further steps ahead

9. The BEM process manifests a growth in unity. Its continuation is a key to further growth into unity. But we still have far to go. We encourage the churches to take further steps together in a partnership of response and dialogue.

10. There are those churches and Christians who have not participated in the BEM process or who have been fundamentally critical of it. We need their contribution and hope to deepen our dialogue with them, for the sake of our common faithfulness to our Lord's prayer that we all may be one, that the world may believe.

11. There are areas of difficulty which remain in need of further clarification and reflection. There are areas of disagreement in understanding and practice which persist despite discussion, study and prayer. These were noted in the responses of many churches. Some examples would be the relation of word and sacrament, the understanding of sacrament and sacramentality, the threefold ministry, succession in ministry, the ministry of men and women, the relation of Scripture and Tradition, and ecclesiology. In rejoicing at the new situation brought about by the responses to BEM we do not minimize the seriousness of these and other questions. They remain issues that keep many of our churches and people apart and they require further work.

12. The issues raised by the churches in their responses have stimulated Faith and Order to initiate a study of ecclesiology. The Commission's major projects on the apostolic faith and on the unity of the church and the

renewal of human community are significant contributions to and participation in the ongoing BEM process.

IV. Seeking fuller visible unity

13. If the affirmations made by the churches in their responses are given their full value we will see an increasing number of practical steps towards unity among the churches. It is still early in this process. The churches may ponder the responses of the other communions and indeed of their own and embody their new understanding in changed relationships. We await this with expectation and a good hope that the churches will act on this opportunity so that the special gift of this moment is not lost.

14. What we are experiencing in the BEM event is an outpouring of God's blessing. We believe the churches are determined to deepen and extend the communion of sharing, celebration, mutual challenge and dialogue which has arisen around BEM. We are full of hope that as the churches study and receive each other's responses to BEM there will be a new season of grace, that the commitments of our common faith which these responses show will lead to acts of unity, deepening of relationships, and community of witness. We ask our churches each to examine whether in the BEM event a way has been opened for them to take new steps towards manifesting our oneness in Christ. We look forward to these steps. We wait in anticipation for the new thing they may make possible in our common life.

15. The BEM process, with all its shortcomings, has shown the impact of ecumenical work on the global level. In this lies its unique ecumenical significance, and certainly its significance for the future work of Faith and Order. It is a specific work of limited scope. It is done slowly, with the pain and patience which such labour demands. It urges us to listen to the other's story with compassion, to share the other's experience with empathy, and to bear the other's burden with mercy. In a renewed and sober hope that does not grow weary we look forward to the way ahead, asking that on that way Christ may be glorified by the church's service of God in the fullness of the Holy Spirit.

16. For all this we ask you to join us in giving thanks to God.

APPENDIX II
Persons Involved in the Preparation of this Report

1. The BEM Steering Group and drafting team, together with staff, have elaborated the present report.

BEM Steering Group
Rev. Prof. Thomas HOPKO, Orthodox Church in America (moderator)
Prof. Torleiv AUSTAD, Church of Norway
Bishop Daniel of Lugojanul (CIOBOTEA), Romanian Orthodox Church
   (since 1989)
Rev. Prof. Akira J. IMAHASHI, United Church of Christ in Japan
Bishop Timotei of Arad (SEVICIU), Romanian Orthodox Church
   (until 1989)
Dr YEOW Choo Lak, Presbyterian Church in Singapore

BEM drafting team
In addition to Prof. Thomas Hopko and Prof. Torleiv Austad:
Prof. Anton HOUTEPEN, Roman Catholic Church, Netherlands
Dom Emmanuel LANNE, OSB, Roman Catholic Church, Belgium
Dr Mary TANNER, Church of England
Prof. Günter WAGNER, Baptist Union, Switzerland
Prof. Geoffrey WAINWRIGHT, Methodist Church in Great Britain
Dr Morris WEST, Baptist Union of Great Britain and Ireland

Faith and Order staff responsible for BEM
Rev. Dr Günther GASSMANN, Evangelical Church in Germany,
   Lutheran
Rev. Dr Irmgard KINDT-SIEGWALT, Evangelical Church in Germany,
   Lutheran (since 1987)
Frère Max THURIAN, Roman Catholic Church (until 1986)

2. In addition to Prof. Austad, Prof. Hopko, Prof. Houtepen, Dr Tanner, Bishop Timotei of Arad, Prof. Wagner, Dr West, Prof. Wainwright, Dr Yeow Choo Lak and staff, the following persons have undertaken preparatory evaluations of specific points in the responses or have assisted in editorial work:

Mrs Eileen CHAPMAN, Presbyterian Church (Administrative Assistant)
Dr (Mrs) Kyriaki FITZGERALD, Greek Orthodox Archiodocese of North and South America/Ecumenical Patriarchate
Father Nicolas GUERIN, Roman Catholic Church, France
Ms Ursula GIESEKE, Evangelical Church in Rhineland, FRG (Intern)
Mrs Beate MAEDER-METCALF, Evangelical Church in Baden, FRG (Intern)
Dr Melanie MAY, Church of the Brethren, USA
Mr Rüdiger NOLL, Evangelical Church of Westphalia (Intern)
Prof. Jude D. WEISENBECK, Roman Catholic Church, USA
Rev. J.-Hinrich WITZEL, Evangelical Lutheran Church of Hanover, FRG (Intern)